SIMONE BILES

GOLDEN GIRL OF GYMNASTICS

Neil Armstrong

Jackie Robinson

Harriet Tubman

Jane Goodall

Albert Einstein

Beyoncé

Stephen Hawking

Simone Biles

>>TRAIL BLAZERS

SIMONE BILES

GOLDEN GIRL OF GYMNASTICS

SALLY J. MORGAN

RANDOM HOUSE 🏠 NEW YORK

Visit us on the Web! rhcbooks.com

Educators and librarians, for a variety of teaching tools, visit us at
RHTeachersLibrarians.com

Library of Congress Cataloging-in-Publication Data
Name: Morgan, Sally J., author.
Title: Trailblazers: Simone Biles: Golden Girl of Gymnastics / by Sally J. Morgan.
Description: New York: Random House Children's Books, 2020 | Series: Trailblazers |
Includes bibliographical references and index.
ISBN 978-0-593-12452-9 (trade pbk.) — ISBN 978-0-593-12453-6 (lib. bdg.)
ISBN 978-0-593-12454-3 (ebook)

Created by Stripes Publishing Limited, an imprint of the Little Tiger Group

Printed in the United States of America
10 9 8 7 6 5 4 3 2 1

First Edition

Contents

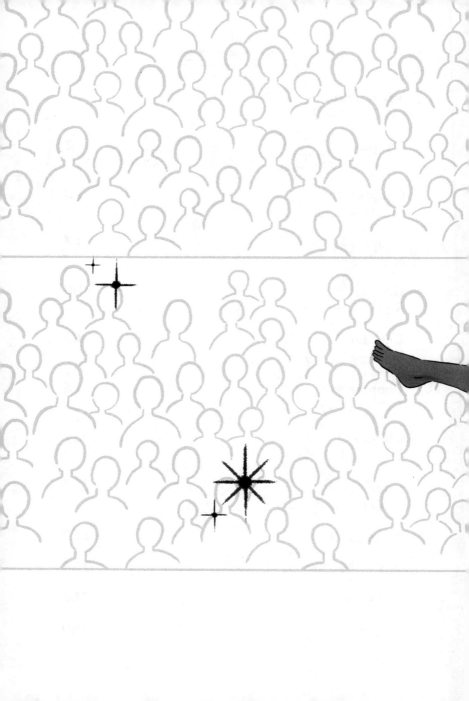

GOING FOR GOLD

On August 11, 2016, a young gymnast took her starting position on the floor in the individual women's all-around final at the Olympic Games in Rio de Janeiro, Brazil. The crowd knew it was about to see something special. The spectators were witnessing history being made. Before them was then three-time world and four-time national all-around champion Simone Biles. The four-foot-eight-inch nineteen-year-old from Spring, Texas, was ninety seconds away from her dream of winning gold coming true.

For a women's artistic gymnast, a medal in the all-around competition is the most highly prized of the six events in the Olympic Games. Only the two highest-scoring gymnasts from each national team are allowed to take part. Simone was on a winning streak, unbeaten in all-around competition since 2013, and she was determined to win again.

Simone had nailed her floor routine in practice countless times, but no matter how often she and her teammates told each other that it was "just like practice" to calm their nerves, pulling off the routine in a competition was different.

The Ancient Olympic Games

The first known Olympic Games were held in 776 BCE in Olympia, Greece—a town named after Mount Olympus, the highest mountain in the country and the mythical

home of many ancient Greek gods and goddesses. To honor the greatest of these gods—Zeus—the Greeks built a sanctuary at Olympia where they could gather and worship him.

Every four years, the best male athletes traveled to Olympia to compete. Women were not allowed to participate or even attend. At first the Olympic Games had just one event—a 600-foot (183 m) running race in the *stadion*, the ancient Greek predecessor of a modern-day stadium. Athletes had to compete naked!

Between 724 BCE and 393 CE, more events were added, including chariot racing, wrestling, boxing, and javelin throwing. The games ended in 393 CE on the orders of the Roman emperor Theodosius I, a Christian who banned all celebration of the ancient gods.

The Modern Olympic Games

The first modern Olympic Games took place in 1896. As with the ancient games, only men were allowed to compete. In the Greek city of Athens, 241 athletes from 14 countries gathered to take part in 43 events, including swimming, shooting, weightlifting, and gymnastics.

Winners in each event received a silver medal, a certificate, and an olive branch. Runners-up received a copper medal, a certificate, and a branch of laurel. Olive and laurel branches were symbols of victory for the ancient Greeks. Unlike in today's Olympics, competitors who came in third received nothing.

The first medalist was an American named James Connolly, who won the triple jump on day one of the games. He was the first Olympic champion in more than 1,500 years. To pay tribute to the ancient games, the face of Zeus was carved on one side of the medal. The Acropolis in Athens, Greece—the site of a number of ancient temples—was engraved on the other side.

WOMEN'S ARTISTIC GYMNASTICS

Women's physical strength and competitive spirit have not always been celebrated. Throughout history, many people believed that being strong and competitive was something only men should aim for. At the turn of the twentieth century, attitudes began to change. As women started to take part in sports, the demand for opportunities to compete increased. Women's events were added to the Olympic Games in 1900; women could compete in tennis, sailing, croquet, golf, and horseback riding.

Around this time, artistic gymnastics grew in popularity. Women saw the activity as a way to keep fit and healthy, and practiced it in social clubs in Europe and the United States. It was also introduced in some schools. The term *artistic* was originally used to differentiate its moves from exercises used by the military. Now there are other types of gymnastics, including rhythmic, where gymnasts use equipment such as a ribbon, a hoop, or a ball as part of their routines.

Women's artistic gymnastics was introduced at the 1928 Olympic Games, held in Amsterdam, the Netherlands. The competition didn't look very much like the one Simone Biles would dominate almost ninety years later. While men competed in seven gymnastics events, women were permitted to take part in just one—the team competition.

In this event, sixty women were divided into five national teams. They competed in three events—drill, apparatuses, and jumps—with the scores across all these events contributing to their final result. Women performed together and were judged for grace, balance, and teamwork rather than for their individual performances. Instead of the formfitting leotards gymnasts compete in today, women gymnasts at the 1928 games wore baggy shorts and shirts. The Netherlands brought home the first women's artistic gymnastics gold medal.

The United States sent its first women's team to the Olympic Games in 1948. The US women took silver in the team event, which was still the only gymnastics competition women were allowed to take part in.

The women's artistic gymnastics competition didn't start to resemble today's until the 1952 games in Helsinki, Finland, when women competed in seven events: individual all-around, team all-around, balance beam, floor exercise, uneven bars, vault, and team portable apparatus (similar to today's Olympic rhythmic gymnastics competition). From small beginnings, women's artistic gymnastics has grown to be one of the most watched sports in the Summer Olympic Games.

Other Competitions

The Olympics isn't the only competition in a gymnast's calendar. For US athletes, there are several other big events, both international and national:

- **World Artistic Gymnastics Championships**
  This competition was first held in Antwerp, Belgium, in 1903, but once again only men were allowed to compete.

A women's team event was added in 1934, as well as a women's individual all-around competition. The championships are held annually in non-Olympic years.

- **US Gymnastics Championships**
  This elite-level national artistic gymnastics competition has been held annually in the US since 1963 and is the national championships for American men's and women's gymnastics. Every fourth year, the competition qualifies top finishers to the US Olympic Team Trials, from which the US Olympic team is determined.

- **US Classic**
  This is an annual summer meet for elite female artistic gymnasts. It is used as a qualifier for the US Gymnastics Championships.

- **American Cup**
  This elite-level international gymnastics event is held annually in the US. It is exclusively an all-around competition.

SIMONE TAKES TO THE FLOOR

The crowd was with Simone from the moment she began her 2016 Olympic floor routine. They clapped along to the rhythmic samba music and cheered as she stuck the landing of each difficult tumbling pass.

Simone smiled at the crowd—she was working hard, but she was also having fun. Gymnastics was her passion and had been since the first time she set foot in a gym at six years old.

> "If I thought of gymnastics as a job, it would put too much stress on me.... At the end of the day, if I can say I had fun, it was a good day."
> —Simone Biles

After Simone's strong performance on the other apparatuses, she needed to score only 13.833 on the floor exercise to take home gold—a relatively easy feat for her. But just as in practice, Simone was determined to do more than was asked of her. As she put it, "If they said, 'Do five pull-ups,' I would always want to do ten."

When Simone's routine ended, the crowd exploded in applause. Simone waved to the audience and ran into the waiting arms of her coach, Aimee Boorman, and teammate Alexandra "Aly" Raisman. Out of a maximum possible score of 16.800, Simone got a massive 15.933! It was more than enough to win her the gold medal and her place in the history books, while Aly took silver.

Simone had proven, yet again, that she was a gymnast unlike any other. The average margin of victory in the individual all-around competition since 1972 is 0.2 points. Simone's final score was more than two full points higher than Aly's and almost four points higher than bronze-medal winner Aliya Mustafina's score. Simone hadn't just won; she had eclipsed the competition.

Her floor routine would have been impossible for almost any other gymnast in history to perform.

But Simone's journey to Olympic gold had been far from easy. Like any athlete, she had worked hard and made big sacrifices to reach her goals. "This has been her destiny all along," one of the commentators announced as Simone left the floor. Perhaps it was true. But Simone had also fought extremely hard for this moment. From training for thirty-two hours a week at the gym to sacrificing what she believed to be "normal" childhood experiences, Simone had put gymnastics first her whole life. All that dedication and hard work had led her to this moment on the podium. Now that she had reached the top, the world wondered what Simone Biles could possibly do next. For a young woman who had chased and achieved impossible goals all her life, it was sure to be something spectacular.

CHAPTER 1

FINDING A HOME

Simone Arianne Biles was born on March 14, 1997, in Columbus, Ohio. She was named by her grandfather Ronald, after one of his favorite singers, Nina Simone. Simone's birth mother, Shanon Biles, had two older children: Ashley, who was seven, and Tevin, who was three. Two years later, another sister, Adria, was born.

Simone's father, Kelvin Clemons, had problems with addiction and did not live with the family. Shanon also struggled with addictions to alcohol and drugs, and didn't have much money to buy food or clothes for her children. Simone and her siblings were often hungry. Sometimes, they had to put water on their cereal because there was no milk. Simone was even mad at a neighborhood cat that she felt was fed more regularly than she was.

≡ FOSTER FAMILY ≡

Shanon's neighbors became concerned. They saw that Simone and her siblings were left to fend for themselves much of the time, and that Shanon didn't seem to be able to take care of them. When Simone was three years old, the neighbors called social services, and a social worker came to visit the house. After seeing the conditions the children were living in and hearing how much they were left on their own, the social worker decided they should go into foster care. She hoped this would give Shanon a chance to recover and get herself in a position to give her children a stable home.

Fostering and Adoption

Foster care provides a temporary home for children whose parents are unable to care for them. A foster family takes in a child, or group of children, for a period of time ranging from a few weeks to several years. Children often return to their parents' care once the problems that caused them to enter foster care have been resolved and their parents are able to look after them safely. Today, more than 400,000 children in the US are in foster care.

Unlike foster care, adoption is permanent. The legal rights of a child's biological parents are transferred to the adoptive parents, who become the child's legal parents permanently. About 135,000 children are adopted in the US each year.

Although I was young when my foster care ordeal began, I remember how it felt to be passed off and overlooked. Like nobody knew me or wanted to know me. Like my talents didn't count, and my voice didn't matter.

Some children in foster care are taken in by other members of their family. Simone's grandfather Ronald lived more than a thousand miles away in Spring, Texas. The social worker called Ronald to tell him what was happening. He started making plans for Simone, Ashley, Tevin, and Adria to live with him and his wife, Nellie, until Shanon was able to look after them herself.

While Ronald was making arrangements, Simone and her sisters and brother went to live with a couple they called Miss Doris and Mr. Leo. Tevin and Ashley missed Shanon a lot, but Simone didn't mind the separation too much. Her foster family had their own children, so there was always someone to play with. She liked knowing that she could expect breakfast every morning and dinner every night, something she had never been sure of before.

Simone enjoyed playing on the swing in the backyard with her brother. Tevin would swing as high as he could before letting go and flipping to the ground. Even though Simone was only three, she was determined to do the same. When it was her turn, Tevin dared her to swing even higher, and Simone was always up for the challenge.

The backyard also had a trampoline, and Simone longed to try some of the acrobatic flips she saw her foster siblings attempting on it. But Simone and the other Biles children weren't allowed. Miss Doris and Mr. Leo were worried about what would happen if Simone or her siblings got hurt while they were looking after them.

Simone may not have been allowed on the trampoline, but that didn't stop her from bouncing around her foster parents' home. She was a bundle of energy and strong for her age—so strong that tiny Simone managed to pull herself up onto the high counter in the kitchen to sneak into the cookie jar and get at a lollipop inside. Her foster mother was amazed. She told Simone never to do it again in case she fell and hurt herself. But the woman was so impressed that she let Simone have the lollipop!

"I remember when she was in foster care, I would go in the house to visit them....You had to walk up three steps into the house, and Simone would jump from the top of the steps into your arms."
—Ronald Biles

⋛ A TRIP TO TEXAS ⋜

Simone and her siblings had been living with Miss Doris and Mr. Leo for just over a year when Ronald came to take them to stay with him in Texas. He hoped he could give them a good home until Shanon got better. Simone, Ashley, Tevin, and Adria said goodbye to their foster parents and went on their first-ever plane ride to Houston.

Ronald lived with his wife, Nellie, on a quiet street called Shady Arbor Lane. Nellie wasn't Shanon's mother, but she treated Simone and her siblings like grandchildren, and Simone called her Grandma.

Ronald and Nellie shared their four-bedroom house with their two sons—Ronald "Ron" Jr., who was sixteen, and Adam, who was fourteen. The house wasn't small, but with four extra children arriving so suddenly, it was a bit of a squeeze!

Simone liked the house right away. Before the children arrived, Nellie's friends had given her furniture and toys to help them settle in. Simone was thrilled to have a bunk bed, her very own set of books, and a scooter. Simone shared the bunk bed with Ashley, and Adria slept in a crib. Tevin shared a room with Adam.

Simone would often swing from the slats on the top bunk or even climb up the side of Adria's crib. She was protective of her little sister and liked to be close to her. Adria followed Simone everywhere until, slowly but surely, she learned to trust Nellie.

The house had a large yard with a trampoline like the one at Miss Doris and Mr. Leo's home, but Simone could jump on this one as much as she wanted! Simone bounced and bounced, trying to copy Ron Jr.'s and Adam's acrobatics. They were impressed that someone so little could jump so high!

I think we felt we were in a fairy tale of our own, because everywhere we looked there were shiny new things that our grandparents thought we'd need.

But it wasn't a complete fairy tale. As happy as Simone was with the trampoline and her shelf full of books, she wasn't happy with what she found on the dinner table. Simone had been used to eating pizza, pasta, and cereal, but her grandma insisted on serving a healthy balance of meat and vegetables. Simone refused to eat the food and even tried to hide it under her booster seat.

Over time, Simone and her grandma came to a compromise. Nellie agreed to mash up the healthy food and serve it alongside food Simone liked, and Simone agreed to try whatever she was given.

⋸ UP IN THE AIR ⋸

After Simone had been living with her grandparents for eight months, Shanon came to visit. Shanon missed her children. She believed she was doing better, and she wanted them to come back to live with her in Ohio. Ronald and Nellie were worried about what would happen to the children if Shanon wasn't able to care for them, but there was nothing they could do. The children flew back to Ohio with their grandpa, but they didn't go to Shanon's house. Instead, they went back to stay with Miss Doris and Mr. Leo. At the time, Simone didn't understand why, but the social worker wanted to make sure Shanon really was better before allowing the children to live with her.

Unfortunately, Shanon was still struggling with addiction and wasn't able to prove she was capable of looking after the children. Simone and her siblings spent another year with their foster family before child services ended Shanon's parental rights; she no longer had a say in what happened to her children. This meant that the Biles siblings were put up for adoption. The older two children—Ashley, now twelve, and Tevin, seven—wanted to stay in Ohio. They had friends in the area, and they didn't want to move too far away from Shanon. The pair went to live with their great-aunt Harriet, Ronald's older sister, who later adopted them.

Simone and Adria had been happy with Ronald and Nellie and wanted to move back to Texas, so on Christmas Eve 2002, they traveled back to Shady Arbor Lane with their grandparents. The following November, after a lengthy adoption process, Simone and Adria's new family became official. Nellie and Ronald, whom they had called Grandma and Grandpa, became Mom and Dad.

> "My road to success began the day my grandfather and his wife officially adopted my sister and me."
> —Simone Biles

Certificate of Adoption

This is to Certify that

Simone Biles

Has been formally adopted

By **Ronald and Nellie Biles**

THE BUSY BILES FAMILY

Life settled down for Simone and Adria. Nellie was worried about how the household would adjust after all the changes, so she signed up the whole family for counseling sessions. She wanted to do everything she could to reassure the girls that they were safe and were there to stay.

Nellie managed a network of nursing homes that the family co-owned, and Ronald, who had served twenty-two years in the air force, traveled around the country installing air traffic control systems. When Ronald and Nellie went to work, Simone and Adria went to a day care program where Ronald and Nellie's older sons, Ron Jr. and Adam, helped out during the summer.

In 2003, the day care scheduled an outing to a local farm, but bad weather that day meant that the children needed to go somewhere indoors instead. Ron Jr., Adam, and the other staff could have gone to a museum or a library, but instead they thought the kids might like to work off their energy at a gym down the street. In their matching blue field-trip shirts, the children made their way to Bannon's Gymnastix.

Inside Bannon's Gymnastix

Bannon's Gymnastix was the perfect place for a field trip. It was filled with trampolines and soft mats and had more than 20,000 square feet of space for the kids to explore. But while it might have looked like a playground to Simone

Bars: Bars are suspended between steel frames in a variety of heights.

Mats: Soft mats ensure a gentler landing for gymnasts to protect their bodies as they learn and perfect their skills.

Sprung floor: The floor is fitted with springs and padding below to give a slight bounce and absorb shock.

nd her friends, Bannon's was actually a world-
lass gymnastics facility, offering training not
nly to children taking their first steps on the
at, but to elite gymnasts ready to participate
n national and international competitions.

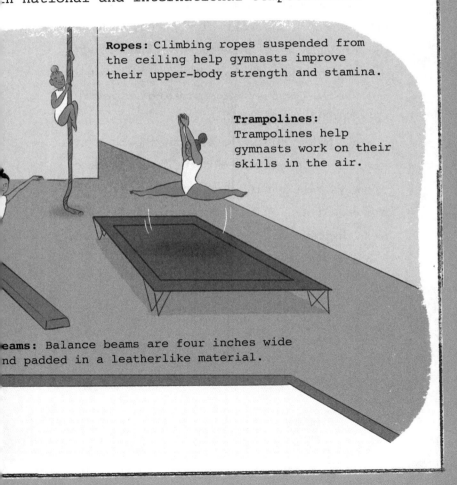

Ropes: Climbing ropes suspended from the ceiling help gymnasts improve their upper-body strength and stamina.

Trampolines: Trampolines help gymnasts work on their skills in the air.

eams: Balance beams are four inches wide
nd padded in a leatherlike material.

Simone watched as gymnasts worked out on the apparatuses, flipping and tumbling. To her, it didn't look so different from what she could do on the trampoline at home, so she started copying some of their moves.

Veronica Banghart, a coach at the gym, couldn't believe her eyes. She asked where Simone had learned the difficult tricks. When she found out Simone hadn't done any training and had just made up the flips on the spot, she gave Simone a letter to take home, inviting her to attend classes at Bannon's.

When Nellie first saw the letter, she thought it must have been sent home with all of the day care children as a way for the gym to sell lessons. But Adam explained that only Simone had been given the note. Nellie decided that gymnastics might be the perfect hobby for two girls with so much energy.

CHAPTER 2

FIRST STEPS ON THE MAT

Nellie signed the girls up for two forty-five minute classes a week. She sent them to their first lesson wearing leotards they had chosen from the gym's pro shop. Simone took to gymnastics classes straightaway. She loved climbing and jumping and had tons of energy, but she also had a lot to learn. Most gymnasts start when they are toddlers, learning forward rolls in parent-and-baby classes. With all the moving between foster care homes in Ohio and Texas, Simone and Adria had never had a chance to take part in those kinds of classes. Compared to many of the children in their gymnastics group, they were quite old to be starting out.

In their first lessons, the girls learned the basic positions of gymnastics. Simone knew how to flip and do cartwheels, but learning the correct way to position her body and point her toes would help polish her skills.

Gymnastics Positions

Layout: The gymnast flips with legs straight, toes pointed, and arms down by their legs.

Pike: The gymnast positions their legs straight ahead of them, points their toes, and stretches their arms toward their toes.

Straddle: The gymnast positions their legs straight and spread wide apart.

Tuck: The gymnast bends at the hips and brings their knees in to their chest.

STANDING OUT

Right from her first few sessions, Simone stood out. She was strong for her age and could do things much older girls struggled to learn, such as pushing herself into a handstand from a seated position. Simone's coach, Veronica, wanted her daughter, Aimee Boorman, who coached the more advanced gymnasts, to watch Simone in action. Aimee was amazed when she spotted Simone executing a perfect seat drop—a trick usually performed on a trampoline—on a mat that was only four inches thick.

"She was waiting for her turn on bars, and she could not stand still. I could see how energetic she was. It was just the kinetic energy from her body, and it was, wow, this kid is something."
—Aimee Boorman

Aimee believed Simone had a special talent. She moved Simone into a group known as the Jet Star Team. There, Simone would be coached alongside the best gymnasts at Bannon's and work through the levels of the USA Gymnastics Junior Olympic (JO) program. Aimee hoped that, after more training, Simone might be ready to compete in regional and eventually national competitions. Gymnasts who do exceptionally well in the JO program can even qualify to compete at the elite level, where they might take part in the World Artistic Gymnastics Championships and the Olympic Games.

THE CHEETAH GIRLS

Simone attended Benfer Elementary School, which was just over two miles from her house. Simone enjoyed school. Her favorite subject was history, and she respected her teachers. Her best friends from school, Marissa and Becca, lived close by. Adria often joined them as they rode their bikes, played dress-up, and acted out scenes from their favorite TV movie, *The Cheetah Girls,* a musical about four girls trying to get a recording contract while at a drama school in New York City. During their games, each of the friends pretended to be one of the characters from the movie. Simone chose to be Galleria, the leader of the band, who likes to speak her mind. In the movie, Galleria was played by an actress named Raven-Symoné.

In September 2005, when Simone was eight years old, the four girls built a fort from wood that had been used to protect windows during a recent hurricane. With a sturdy roof and a bench running along one side, the fort was the perfect place for the girls to practice their *Cheetah Girls* routines. One day, while the girls were singing, a fifth and very unwelcome guest came to join them—a spider, which landed right on Marissa's head. Marissa ran out of the fort screaming, with Simone, Adria, and Becca following close behind. None of them wanted to play in the fort much after that!

≳ FAMILY FUN ≲

Simone and Adria came up with all kinds of ways
to entertain themselves. They played soccer in the
yard and drove around in their child-sized motorized
vehicles. The "Trying Not to Laugh" game was a
favorite funny pastime. To play, one sister had to
fill her mouth with water and try to hold it there for
thirty seconds while the other sister tried to make her
laugh—usually with very messy consequences.

Ron Jr. and Adam were in their twenties, but that
didn't mean they didn't have fun with their sisters.
Adam helped his parents by driving the girls to school
every day. At home, they challenged Simone to see how
quickly she could climb up onto their shoulders.

"Simone was a daring girl; she would do anything. If her brothers told her she couldn't do something or challenged her, she would prove to them that she could."
—Nellie Biles

LEARNING THE ROPES

Simone was daring at the gym, too. A few weeks after she started lessons, Bannon's held a recital. Friends and family were invited to see what the gymnasts were working on. For one of the displays, the gymnasts were supposed to climb ten feet of rope using just their arms, with their legs out in front of them. This wasn't enough of a challenge for Simone. Simone kept climbing higher and higher until she was twenty feet off the ground! She had to be told to get down.

The JO program has ten levels, and Simone was quickly progressing through them. Within just a few weeks of her first class, Simone had already mastered the skills required in the first three levels. From her performance at the recital, it was clear to her coaches that Simone had more to give. After her impressive demonstration on the ropes, Simone began learning level-four skills, and it wasn't long before she moved on to level five.

The USA Gymnastics Junior Olympic Program

The JO program is the main gymnastics program for women in the United States. It is made up of ten levels. Gymnasts must be able to perform all the skills in each level before they can move on to the next. Levels one and two focus on some of the most basic moves in gymnastics on four pieces of apparatus—vault, beam, floor, and bars. These skills include performing a cartwheel to side handstand dismount on beam, as well as a back hip circle on the low bar. Gymnasts at levels one and two do not take part in competitions.

Star Move

Back hip circle: The gymnast pushes up on their arms so that the bar is level with their hips. Keeping their arms straight and their toes pointed, the gymnast turns counterclockwise around the bar through 360 degrees.

At levels three and four, gymnasts perform compulsory routines on each of the four apparatuses, also called events. Bar routines are performed on the low bar, and vaults are performed by gymnasts leaping from the springboard onto a stack of mats. Other skills include a cartwheel and a split jump on beam, and a roundoff back handspring on floor. To pass level three and all higher levels, gymnasts must take part in competitions.

<u>Star Move</u>

Roundoff back handspring: A roundoff is similar to a cartwheel, but the gymnast brings both of their feet down at the same time. The gymnast uses the power generated by the roundoff to propel them into a handspring, where they flip backward, arching their back to land on their hands. The gymnast then pushes off with their hands while swinging their legs over their head to land on the mat.

In levels five and six, judges are looking for gymnasts to perform more complex routines cleanly and safely. A key skill at level six is swinging between the high and low bars on the uneven bars, known as a transition.

HEAD OVER HEELS

It was hard for the gym to keep up with Simone. She was always eager to learn new skills and, unlike most gymnasts, she didn't take very long to master them. When Simone was seven, she saw a cheerleader who was visiting the gym perform a backflip (known as a back tuck). Simone told Aimee and the other coaches that she was sure she could do the same move. Aimee didn't believe her, so Simone proved her point by performing a standing back tuck right there. Impressed, another of the coaches, named Susan, challenged her to do it again, this time on the beam. Simone was so confident that she walked straight up to the full-height beam—which was taller than she was—and pulled herself up. The coaches rushed over to stop her—it was too dangerous! Coach Susan told Simone to try it on the floor beam instead. Simone climbed down and performed her back tuck on the floor beam. The coaches were amazed.

"You know how some people have incredible balance? Well, imagine having balance without your feet on the ground while flipping and twisting and knowing exactly when you have to bring your feet down to the floor so that you don't die."
– Aimee Boorman

⇒ SIMONE'S SUPERPOWER ⇐

Simone was naturally muscular and very strong—so strong that she set a school record for doing one hundred push-ups! But sometimes Simone found it hard to concentrate in class, as she didn't like sitting still or focusing on one thing at a time. Simone says she never felt different from the other kids in her class but did find that she always wanted to be busy. When Simone was nine years old, she discovered the reason why. She was diagnosed with **attention deficit hyperactivity disorder (ADHD)**.

> The challenges we face help define who we are. My challenge is also my superpower: ADHD.

Attention Deficit Hyperactivity Disorder

ADHD is a medical condition that affects a person's attention and self-control. Children with ADHD may find it difficult to sit still or stop themselves from interrupting others when speaking. Children with ADHD sometimes have trouble at school, because the disorder can make it hard for them to concentrate or complete tasks. Difficulties controlling impulses can also get students with ADHD in trouble with teachers for disrupting the classroom.

MICHAEL JORDAN

The younger a person with ADHD is diagnosed with the condition, the sooner that person can get the necessary help to achieve their goals.

Simone isn't the only sports legend to be diagnosed with ADHD. Basketball superstar Michael Jordan and the most decorated Olympic medalist of all time, swimmer Michael Phelps, have both spoken out about having the condition.

MICHAEL PHELPS

⧹ UNEVEN GROUND ⧸

At the time Simone was in the JO program, all gymnasts in levels one to six had to perform exactly the same skills on each of the apparatuses. From level seven—now level six—onward, gymnasts choreograph their own routines and get more freedom to pick and choose which skills they perform. Simone was excited to move on to these advanced levels, but there was one obstacle in her way—the uneven bars.

Like most gymnasts, Simone found performing on some apparatuses easier than others. Simone's least favorite event was the uneven bars. Simone even considered continuing in gymnastics without pursuing bars, but she wouldn't be able to compete in the all-around competition if she did so. Coach Aimee believed that if Simone worked hard, she would be able to master the bars, but it wasn't going to be easy. One of the reasons Simone found the uneven bars challenging was because she was short for her age. She therefore had to reach farther to catch the bar on releases than taller gymnasts did.

"The only thing I've ever been truly afraid of in gymnastics—apart from letting everyone down—was that high bar."
—Simone Biles

All Around the Apparatus:
The Uneven Bars

Specifications: Low bar 5.6 ft. (1.7 m)
High bar 8.2 ft. (2.5 m)
Spaced 6 ft. (1.8 m) apart

On this piece of equipment, gymnasts must perform a variety of skills, including daring release moves where they let go of the bar before flying and catching either the same bar or the opposite one. There is no time limit set on the bar, but routines usually last between 30 and 45 seconds. Judges look for body position and for each of the elements to flow from one to the next without pauses. Dismounts often include exciting flips and twists before the gymnast lands with both feet on the mat at the same time with no additional hops or steps.

Star Move

Kip: The gymnast holds the bar and swings forward before pulling her feet up in a pike position. The gymnast then pulls herself up to bring her hips level with the bar.

CRASH LANDING

Another reason Simone was scared of the uneven bars was that she'd had a nasty fall. When she was learning a skill called a giant, her hands slipped off the high bar. Simone landed hard on the floor. She wasn't too badly hurt, but the fall shook her confidence.

She told her uneven-bars coach, Nicole, that she would never do it again. Coach Nicole wouldn't let her quit. She picked up Simone and lifted her back onto the bar. The coach guided Simone through revolution after revolution, until she was sure Simone could do it by herself. By the end of practice, Simone had mastered the giant.

Star Move

Giant: Holding on to the bar, a gymnast rotates 360 degrees with the body in a straight position.

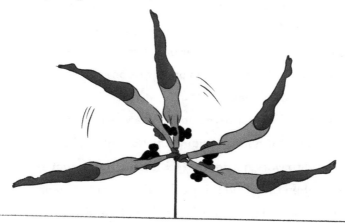

⋛ STUMBLING THROUGH SEVEN ⋛

At level six (level seven when Simone was competing), gymnasts must perform a certain number of skills in varying difficulty levels on each of the apparatuses. They can choose the skills that best suit them and combine them into their own routines, allowing for more creativity. Key skills at this level include a giant on bars; tumbling sequences on floor that connect skills in a row, like a roundoff back handspring to a backflip; and a flight skill on the beam, such as a back handspring or a roundoff.

Even though Simone had mastered the giant, level seven still managed to slip from her grasp. Simone failed her first attempt at passing the level, and not just because of her performance on bars. She muddled her landings on her floor routines and wobbled on the beam.

Although Simone was upset, she was determined to never let it happen again. She had talent, but she needed to work harder and to listen to her coaches, even when they said things she didn't want to hear. Simone's hard work and focus paid off, and she passed at her very next competition.

CHAPTER 3

NEW MOVES

After Benfer Elementary School, Simone went to Strack Intermediate School along with Marissa. Although she had friends, she wasn't one of the "cool kids" at school. Simone was naturally muscular as a child, and her gymnastics training made her even stronger. Some of the kids in her class were mean and nicknamed her "Swolger," a combination of *swollen*, in reference to the size of her muscles, and *soldier*, because her muscles made her look tough. Simone tried not to let it bother her, but she couldn't help feeling self-conscious. She wore baggy clothes and bulky jackets to try to make her muscles less obvious.

One place Simone didn't try to hide her strength was on the soccer field at recess. The boys at Strack told the girls they weren't allowed to join the game, but Simone and her friend Megan started playing anyway. Unimpressed, some of the boys kicked them in the shins to get the girls to leave. Simone simply kicked them back and kept on playing!

SETTING GOALS

As Simone climbed the levels of the JO program, she took part in more and more competitions. At first she competed in local events, but soon she added statewide competitions, where she often beat gymnasts several years older than she was. Some coaches had concerns that she was moving too fast, but Simone loved it. So long as Simone was having fun, neither Aimee nor Simone's parents saw any reason to stop her.

"I never felt as if my parents were forcing me to keep going."
—Simone Biles

At the start of each year, Nellie encouraged Simone to write down her goals for the future. Her list for that year might have looked something like this:

MY GOALS

Become an elite gymnast.
Be selected for the national team.
Compete in the Olympic Games.
Go to prom.
Go to UCLA on a gymnastics scholarship.
Meet Zac Efron.

The next Olympic Games would be held in London, England, in 2012, but Simone wouldn't be old enough to take part. Olympic rules state that athletes must turn sixteen in that calendar year to compete. In 2012, Simone would only be fifteen and wouldn't turn sixteen until the following March. She was going to have to wait until the next games, in 2016, when she would be nineteen. She worried that she would be too old by then or that she could become injured. Although there is no upper age restriction in gymnastics, most female gymnasts are at their peak of power and flexibility at about sixteen years old. The oldest member of the US team who competed in 2012 was eighteen.

An Unbreakable Record

In 1996, Dominique Moceanu became the youngest US gymnast to win a gold medal in the Olympic Games. At just fourteen years old, Dominique helped her team win gold at the games in Atlanta. The record is unlikely to be beaten, because the Fédération Internationale de Gymnastique (FIG)—the governing body for world gymnastics—raised the age for competing in the Olympic Games to sixteen in 1997. The rules were changed to protect young gymnasts from injury and to allow them to develop the mental stamina needed to compete at such a high level.

A FURRY GOOD INCENTIVE

In addition to encouraging her to set goals, Simone's parents also gave her incentives to do well in competitions. Simone and Adria longed for a dog and asked for one every Christmas, but Nellie and Ronald held back on getting them a pet.

In 2008, Simone made a deal with her dad. If, in her

next regional qualifier, her score was high enough to make it into the Western Championships, Ronald would get them a dog. The Western Championships was an important competition because it would mean the chance to compete with the best level-nine gymnasts in the nation.

That was the extra push Simone needed. She performed well in the competition. When she looked up at the scoreboard and saw that she had qualified, she was happy about making the cut—but she was even happier that she would finally be getting a dog! Simone and Adria named their new German shepherd puppy Maggie Elena Biles and loved her very much.

Elite Gymnasts

Having completed level nine, Simone was able to choreograph her own routines, using skills from a book called the *Code of Points*, a manual that contains guidance on what a gymnast's routine must include, along with a difficulty score for each of these elements. The book also contains direction for judges on how to award scores for execution.

Few gymnasts reach level ten due to the amount of training and commitment required to learn the necessary skills. After level ten, a gymnast must decide whether they want to try to progress to the elite level, which is even more advanced.

Elite gymnastics is divided into two ranks: national and international. Teams for the Olympic Games and the World Artistic Gymnastics Championships are chosen from the international rank.

NEW HOME, NEW SCHOOL

A new dog wasn't the only change for the Biles family—they were moving. Their new home had a swimming pool and enough bedrooms for Simone and Adria to each have her own. Simone planned to decorate her room with posters of her favorite gymnasts and as much zebra print as possible.

The downside of moving was that their new house was farther away from Simone's school and gym. Simone was spending about twenty hours a week training at Bannon's Gymnastix. If she wanted to get better, she would need to spend even more time there. The extra time it would take her to get to the gym would make that impossible. Simone would have to change schools.

In 2008, Simone transferred to a private school opposite Bannon's. Simone was happy that she could spend more time in the gym, but she didn't like her new school. Not only were all her friends back at Strack, but some of her classmates and teachers couldn't seem to learn her name, with one teacher even calling her "Somalia" for an entire year. Simone held on to the fact that she would only be there until eighth grade. After that, she planned to go to public high school and be reunited with her friends.

⋛ LIFE AT LEVEL TEN ⋚

Now a level-ten gymnast, Simone placed third in the
individual all-around competition and won first place
in two other events at the 2010 Houston National
Invitational competition. At the end of the meet,
Simone discovered she had won five thousand dollars.
She was presented with a check, but she didn't want
to touch it. Simone knew that if she accepted money
for competing in gymnastics, it would mean she had
"gone professional," which would make her ineligible to
compete in college gymnastics (and that, along with
going to high school and competing at the Olympics, was
high on her list of goals). Her dad explained to Simone
that she could accept the check on behalf of her gym.

BANK ◥		
		CHECK NO. ___ 01.
PAY	Simone Biles	
		DATE ___ 201
THE SUM OF	$5,000.00	
		AUTH SIGN
BANK ◥	6789 - 134526789 - 1231234	

PROFESSIONAL VS. AMATEUR

Colleges often offer financial aid in the form of scholarships to attract talented athletes to join their sports teams. Many gymnasts see these scholarships as a way to get a good education, which can be very expensive, while still being able to compete in the sport they love. According to the National Collegiate Athletic Association (NCAA) rules, professional athletes—defined as those who make money out of their athletic abilities—are not allowed to compete in college athletics. In order for gymnasts to qualify for a scholarship and compete in college sports, they cannot have earned money through sponsorship or competitions. For gymnasts, this means giving up the chance of profiting from their sport when they are at their very best.

Some people argue that the rules should be changed for gymnasts, who, unlike football or baseball players, are unlikely to make a living from their sport after college. There are no major-league teams looking to sign up gymnasts after graduation, and even if there were, gymnasts are at the peak of their careers during their teens and early twenties.

At level ten, coaches and judges pay a lot more attention to how gymnasts perform. When Simone was a level-ten gymnast, she attracted the attention of national team coordinator Márta Károlyi.

Márta Károlyi

Márta Károlyi began her career in Romania, where she and her husband, Béla, set up a gymnastics training school. There, they coached Romanian gymnast Nadia Comăneci, world and Olympic gold medalist. The Károlyis moved to the US in 1981 and set up the Károlyi Ranch in Huntsville, Texas (see page 69), which became the USA Gymnastics National Team Training Center.

Márta Károlyi

Márta introduced the training methods they used in their world-famous gymnastics school in Romania to the US. The training style of Márta and Béla is known for being tough and uncompromising—but it got results, producing teams such as the Magnificent Seven, the Fierce Five, and the Final Five team that completed in Rio in 2016.

Aimee hoped Simone's performance in Houston would be enough to secure an invite to train with Márta. She sent Márta videos of Simone's routine, but the national team coordinator pointed out Simone's weak performance on bars and turned her down.

Nellie began to wonder if it was Simone's coaching that was stopping her from performing at her best. Aimee had been a wonderful coach so far, but perhaps she had brought Simone as far as she could go. Aimee had been a gymnast but was forced to give up the sport at level eight following an injury. Aimee reassured Nellie that she believed she could take Simone as far as Simone wanted to go, and if there was anything she didn't think she could teach Simone, she would bring in people who could.

⇒ ANOTHER CHANCE ⇐

Aimee did as she'd said and brought in extra coaches. She and Simone worked together on her bar routine for hours on end. With the additional help, Simone made it to the elite level and earned a spot at a training camp with Márta Károlyi herself.

At camp, Simone was surrounded by some of the best gymnasts in the country. Márta noticed Simone practicing and liked what she saw, but she thought Simone could push herself further. Márta told Aimee that she wanted to see Simone perform one of the most difficult vaults in gymnastics in competition—a vault known as the Amanar. Simone wasn't so sure.

All Around the Apparatus: Vault

Specifications: Runway: length: 78—82 ft.
(23.8—25 m); width: 3.2 ft. (1 m)
Table: height: 4 ft. (1.2 m);
length: 3—3.5 ft. (0.9—1.1 m);
width: 3 ft. (0.9 m)

A gymnast sprints down a runway before
hitting the springboard with either
their hands or feet. The gymnast uses the
springboard to propel themselves onto the
table before pushing off into the air.
Judges look for speed, height, and body
position during the various flips and twists
the gymnast completes while soaring above
the table. The judges also look for a clean
landing in which both feet hit the mat at
the same time with no hops.

Star Move

The Amanar: First performed by Simona
Amânar at the 2000 Olympic Games in
Sydney, Australia.

After sprinting down the runway, a gymnast
performs:

1. a roundoff onto the springboard
2. a back handspring onto the
   vaulting table
3. two and a half twists in the air with
   body fully extended
4. a blind landing (the gymnast
   is unable to see the mat as she
   comes in to land)

Simone's next chance to impress Márta was at the 2011 US Championships in Saint Paul, Minnesota. The top thirteen gymnasts at the competition would be invited to attend more training camps with Márta and stood the chance of being considered for the US Junior National Team.

Simone had trained hard, but she didn't want to perform the Amanar. She'd done it in practice many times, but she didn't think she was ready to do it in a competition. She was scared that she wouldn't be able to land the vault safely and might injure or embarrass herself. Instead, Simone chose a vault she felt sure she could land cleanly. Her chosen vault wasn't as difficult as the Amanar, but if she performed it well, it might just be enough to get her in the top thirteen.

Things didn't go as planned. Instead of sticking the landing, Simone hopped backward. At the end of the competition, she watched the scoreboard to see who had made the top thirteen. Simone had placed fourteenth. She had missed her shot at camp by just one spot. Simone was heartbroken and felt she had let everyone down.

GYMNASTICS VS. NORMAL LIFE

Simone reviewed her performance with Aimee. Together they watched the videos of each event over and over, comparing her routines with those of the top thirteen. Simone could see the difference. The other gymnasts' routines were not only more difficult but also more cleanly executed. Simone was going to have to train harder and increase the difficulty level if she had a hope of beating these girls. But how could she? Simone was already in the gym every spare moment she had.

In fact, soon there would be even less time. Simone was due to start high school in the fall. She was excited to be in classes with Marissa again and wanted to join all the clubs and societies she could. She'd even started to plan her outfit for her first day.

Simone's parents told her there was no way she could spend more time in the gym and go to public school. Elite-level gymnasts have to travel all over the country to attend competitions, and there was the possibility of traveling internationally, too. The school district was strict about how many days a student could miss.

If Simone wanted to succeed as an elite gymnast, she would have to be homeschooled.

Simone didn't know what to do. She wanted a normal high school life with her friends, but after so narrowly missing a spot on the national team, she also wanted to see how far she could go as a gymnast. Simone would have to decide which she wanted more. Her parents told her they didn't care which path she chose and that it was a decision only she could make.

CHAPTER 4

BIG DECISIONS

Simone decided to give homeschooling a try. She hoped the extra hours in the gym would help her make the national team. If that plan didn't work out, she reasoned, she could join her friends in public school for tenth grade. Until then she could see her friends in her free time and stay in touch on social media. If she *did* make the team, then she would have not only the gymnastics career she had worked so hard for but also the opportunity to go to college on a gymnastics scholarship.

HARD LESSONS

The teacher Nellie had in mind was none other than Simone's dad, Ronald. Ronald had retired from working with air traffic control systems and had the time to tutor Simone between her gym sessions. Simone would also take classes online.

Things didn't go as smoothly as Nellie had hoped. Simone and her dad argued about lessons and got on each other's nerves. Ronald thought Simone complained too much, and Simone didn't like her dad telling her what to do. Also, the online classes weren't as flexible as they had hoped. The program required students to do their work and be online at set times, which always seemed to coincide with when Simone needed to be in the gym. In middle school Simone had been a good student, getting As and Bs, but after six weeks of homeschooling, she was getting Fs.

Nellie decided that it would be best for everyone if Simone was taught by Miss Heather, a teacher who worked at the gym, instead. Miss Heather worked at Bannon's three days a week, tutoring gymnasts between their training sessions. On the other days, the gymnasts worked on assignments Miss Heather gave them. Simone liked this arrangement much better. Miss Heather made sure all the gymnasts were learning at the same rate as their public-school peers, and Simone's grades improved quickly.

⇒ MAKING THE TEAM ⇐

Homeschooling meant that Simone could increase her training time in the gym from twenty-five hours a week to more than thirty. The results quickly started to show. In May 2012, Simone got the chance to compete in front of Márta again at the Károlyi Ranch. This time, Simone was determined to perform the Amanar and show the national team coach what she could do. She performed the difficult move perfectly and placed first on vault.

Simone's vault performances had become so strong that she took first place in vault in every competition she entered in 2012, including the US Classic in Chicago and the 2012 Visa Championships in St. Louis, Missouri. At the end of the championships, the USAG selection committee revealed the names of the gymnasts who had made the junior national team. Simone was thrilled to discover she was one of only six junior gymnasts selected for the team, and the only gymnast who had not been on the team the previous year.

⋝ LIFE ON THE RANCH ⋜

As a member of the national team, Simone now had to attend a four-day training camp once a month with Márta at the Károlyi Ranch. Simone had been to competitions at the ranch and the developmental camp the previous year, but this time was different: she was there as a member of the national team. Luckily for Simone and Aimee, it was only a one-hour drive from Spring to Huntsville, but other members of the team flew in from all over the country.

The Károlyi Ranch

The Károlyi Ranch, located deep in the woods of the Sam Houston National Forest, was owned and operated by Béla and Márta Károlyi, the famous coaches of Romanian gymnast Nadia Comăneci and US gymnast Mary Lou Retton.

In addition to hosting gymnastic camps, the ranch was the official national team training site from 2000 to 2018. Members of the national team, as well as other elite gymnasts, traveled with their coaches from all over the US to train with the Károlyis at the ranch in Walker County, Texas, 70 miles outside Houston, for four days every month.

The ranch was home to a 40-acre gymnastics training facility consisting of three fully equipped gymnasiums and a number of basic dormitories, called motels, for gymnasts and their coaches. The ranch was also home to animals, including donkeys, peacocks, and camels.

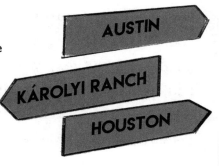

Life at the ranch wasn't easy. The training sessions were tough, the accommodations were basic, and the food wasn't good. Because Simone lived so close, she brought things from home to make her life at the ranch more comfortable, but other gymnasts didn't have that option. Márta expected perfection from her gymnasts, and the hard work required to achieve it. After all, she and her husband, Béla, had coached the very first gymnast to have achieved a perfect score, Nadia Comăneci.

A Perfect Ten

Romanian gymnast Nadia Comăneci's performance on the uneven bars at the 1976 Olympic Games in Montreal was the first time anyone had achieved a perfect 10 in the sport. Nadia went on to receive six more perfect scores in the same games and took home a total of five medals—three gold, one silver, and one bronze. As nobody had achieved a 10 before, the scoreboard only had space for a single digit followed by two decimal places, so her actual score on the day read 1.00.

The scoring system in gymnastics was changed in 2004. Now gymnasts are awarded a combined score—one score for the difficulty of the routine (the D score) and one for how well the gymnast executes the routine (the E score). The D score for an Amanar vault from 2013 to 2016 was 6.3, which, combined with 10 points for perfect execution, means that the highest score a gymnast could have achieved performing a perfect Amanar was 16.3. Gymnasts rarely achieve perfect marks for execution, as tenths of a point are deducted for errors such as bent knees, flexed feet, or hops on the landing.

⋜ OLYMPIC DREAMS ⋜

Simone and her friends watched many of the 2012 Olympic gymnastics events on a big screen set up at Bannon's. She had trained with several members of the Fierce Five, the name chosen by the five female gymnasts competing on the Olympic team. Simone made a promise to herself that she was going to do everything she could to get to the 2016 Olympic Games.

The Fierce Five

GABRIELLE "GABBY" DOUGLAS
Born: December 31, 1995
Gabby won gold in the individual all-around competition at the London 2012 Olympic Games and became the first African American to win the title.
Star events: bars and floor

MCKAYLA MARONEY

Born: December 9, 1995

McKayla is known for being able to perform one of the best Amanar vaults of all time. She won silver in the vault competition at the 2012 Olympic Games.

Star event: vault

ALEXANDRA "ALY" RAISMAN

Born: May 25, 1994

Aly won gold on floor in the 2012 Olympic Games with her incredible tumbling passes; she also won bronze on beam.

Star event: floor

JORDYN WIEBER

Born: July 12, 1995

Winner of the all-around competition at the 2011 world championships, Jordyn narrowly missed out on taking part in the Olympic individual all-around because of a rule that only the two highest scorers from each national team can enter the competition.

Star event: floor

KYLA ROSS

Born: October 24, 1996

Kyla's strong performance on beam helped Team USA win gold in the team competition. Three months shy of 16 years old, Kyla was the youngest member of the Fierce Five.

Star event: beam

⋛ FALLING FROM BEAM ⋛

Simone trained hard at Bannon's and at the ranch, where she was surrounded by stars from the Olympic team. In March 2013, Simone got a chance to prove herself nationally when she was chosen to compete in the American Cup, which was being held at the DCU Center in Worcester, Massachusetts.

The American Cup was a very big tournament for a gymnast on her first national assignment. There were lots of spectators, and the competition would be broadcast on television across the country. Usually, Simone enjoyed competitions as a chance to show off what she had practiced a thousand times in training. But at the American Cup, she was competing in front of—and against—gymnasts she had admired for years. On the competition day, the pressure got to her, and Simone felt sick with nerves. She performed well in her vault, bars, and floor routine but came apart on beam. She stumbled through the moves, lacking her usual grace, and then fell off.

All Around the Apparatus: Balance Beam

Specifications: Length: 16.4 ft. (5 m)
Width: 4 in. (10.2 cm)
Height: 4.1 ft. (1.25 m)

At competitions, gymnasts complete a
90-second routine using the whole length
of the padded beam. Routines include
a variety of jumps, leaps, spins, and
holds, as well as dance and acrobatic
elements.

To complete the routine, a gymnast
performs a dismount. The most important
part of any dismount is the landing.
Ideally both feet land on the mat at the
same time with no added hops. This is
known as "sticking the landing."

A gymnast who falls from the apparatus
during a routine has 30 seconds to climb
back on to avoid disqualification, but
the competitor will be docked a whole
point for the fall.

Simone scrambled back onto the beam in time to complete her set. She performed her dismount well, but as she walked over to Aimee, Simone wanted to cry. She had fallen off the beam on national television. She had fallen in front of world-famous gymnasts. Worst of all, she had fallen in front of Márta, who had trusted her with a spot on the team.

After the American Cup, things started to come apart for Simone in training, too. She argued with Aimee and didn't take her practice sessions seriously. She wasn't used to the regimented training of the national team. Gymnastics had always been fun for her, but now it felt overwhelming.

⸗ PULLED FROM COMPETITION ⸗

Simone needed to find her focus during training if she was going to build up the strength and stamina to make it through the season. But Simone couldn't concentrate and instead found herself arguing with her coaches and not doing what she was told to do. By July, when Simone took part in the US Classic in Chicago, the strain was starting to show.

On uneven bars, Simone fell, almost landing on her face.

On beam, Simone wobbled on her wolf turn (a move where the gymnast spins on one foot in a squat position with the other leg outstretched) and stumbled through the rest of her routine, looking like she could fall off at any minute.

On floor, she landed one tumbling pass on her knees and another so hard she hurt her ankle.

Simone tried to shake it off as she moved on to vault, but Aimee could see that Simone wasn't concentrating. Simone had hurt herself on floor, and Aimee worried she would injure herself further on vault. Aimee decided that Simone should not take part in the vault rotation—she was pulling her from the meet.

Simone was devastated. She knew her performance had not been up to the standard she was capable of, but she couldn't figure out how to set things right.

⋝ YOU CAN DO BETTER ⋜

After the US Classic in Chicago, Márta invited Simone
to a one-on-one training session at the ranch. Simone
was surprised to discover that Márta wasn't angry
at her. She told Simone that she believed in her and
that disastrous competitions are just something that
happens. But, she said, Simone needed to get her head
straight if she wanted to be the best she could be.

> I know you can
> do better, Simone,
> because I've seen
> you do it!

CHAPTER 5

THE START OF A STREAK

It wasn't just Márta and Aimee who could see Simone was struggling; her parents could, too. They wanted to find someone to help, so they did some research and made Simone an appointment with sports psychologist Robert Andrews.

"She was competing against these girls who were her heroes, her idols . . . it was hard for her to adjust to that. Simone didn't think she was good enough to compete with them. I knew she was quite capable. But she needed to believe it."
—Nellie Biles

At first, Simone didn't want to see a psychologist. A gymnast at camp had told her that only crazy people went to see psychologists, and Simone didn't want people to think she was crazy. For the first half of her appointment, she sat hunched in her chair, shrugging her way through the questions that Robert asked her.

Sports Psychology

Many athletes seek help from sports psychologists to overcome issues that might be holding them back from giving their best performance.

In addition to talk therapy, in which the athlete and doctor discuss issues that may be affecting performance, psychologists also give athletes exercises to help them stay calm and focused. These can include visualization exercises, in which athletes imagine themselves performing at their best, and relaxation exercises to help athletes settle their nerves.

Sports psychologists may work with not only the athlete but also their coaches and family members to make sure everyone has the tools they need to help the athlete perform to the best of their abilities.

To put her at ease, Robert listed some of the athletes he had worked with in the past and what they had gone on to achieve. As he spoke, Simone started to listen. These were real athletes who had grappled with pressure, just like she did, but had gone on to do incredible things. She decided that perhaps seeing a psychologist wasn't such a bad idea after all.

As the sessions went on, Simone and Robert discovered what was holding her back. Gymnastics had stopped being fun. Instead of going out and having a good time during her routines, Simone had begun to worry about what people would think of her and what would happen if she let people down.

"I had to convince her to take her foot off the gas, enjoy the game again. She was so stoic at meets. It didn't look like she was having fun. Once she began injecting that Simone smile into her floor routine, the fans and judges started smiling, too."
—Robert Andrews

⋛ HAVING FUN ⋚

Three weeks later, in Hartford, Connecticut, Simone took part in the 2013 US Gymnastics Championships. When she was asked by a reporter what she expected from the national championships competition, Simone said she wanted to "go out there and compete and have fun." Simone smiled throughout her floor routine, making it look easy. It was clear from her confident performance across all the apparatuses that she had put what happened at the US Classic in Chicago behind her. She was ready to compete, and she was ready to win—and she took home gold in the individual all-around competition and silver in the other four events.

Winning the US Gymnastics Championships was just so fun and exciting!

Simone had come back from disaster to prove
she was the best gymnast in the United States, but
how would she fare at an international competition?
Simone was about to find out. She was selected
to compete in the 2013 world championships in
Antwerp, Belgium. It was a chance to prove herself
against more than 130 elite gymnasts from twenty-
four countries, in front of eighteen thousand
spectators.

Before the competition, Márta had told Simone
that since nobody knew who she was yet, she had
nothing to lose. This helped calm Simone's nerves.
To steady herself throughout the competition,
Simone made a point of keeping Márta in her sights
before she started each of her routines. Simone
kept her cool and dazzled the crowd, with one NBC
commentator saying, "I just think she lights up this
whole building."

If people didn't know who Simone Biles was
before her floor routine, they certainly did after.
During her gold medal–winning, ninety-second
performance, she became the first gymnast ever to
perform a double flip in layout position with a half
twist. Simone and Aimee had come up with the move

when Simone was finding that landing a double flip aggravated a calf injury. Adding the half twist made the landing more difficult in terms of skill but didn't cause her any pain. When Márta had seen Simone perform the tumbling move in practice, she'd been impressed.

If you land it in competition, you'll get that move named after you.

All Around the Apparatus: Floor

Specification: Area: 40 ft. x 40 ft. (12.2 m x 12.2 m)

The floor routine is performed to music selected by the gymnast and their coaches. It is a gymnast's chance to show their personality and creativity, as well as demonstrate their skill and power during the 90-second routine, blending choreography with powerful tumbling, turns, and leaps. Judges assess penalties for stepping outside of the marked area.

Star Move

The Biles: After a few running steps, the gymnast performs a roundoff into a back handspring. They use the power generated by these moves to perform a double layout with a half twist, turning their body to face the opposite direction in a blind landing.

BEST GYMNAST IN THE WORLD

Simone nailed the landing of the new skill, and it was later named "the Biles," just as Márta had told her it would be. She performed well in all the events. Her stellar performance on floor won her the gold medal, her vault secured her a silver, and her balance beam won bronze. She even managed to place fourth on uneven bars. Her consistency across all the events won her gold in the all-around. Simone couldn't believe what was happening. She had won medals before, but never at the world championships! Aimee had told her that she needed to shake hands with the bronze and silver medalists, but there were so many things to get right. She watched Kyla Ross—her friend and teammate and an Olympic gold medalist—to see what she should do. The year 2013 had been a roller coaster, but Simone had come out on top of the world.

⌇ TOUGH SKIN ⌇

Simone was brought back down to earth with a bump when she opened Twitter after returning to the United States. Italian gymnast Carlotta Ferlito had made a racist comment in an interview following the competition. She suggested that she and a teammate should "paint our skin black so we can win, too." The media exploded after the incident. Everyone wanted to know how Simone would react, but Simone didn't let the comment get her down.

"It went viral, but it didn't bother me one bit....I guess I just have really tough skin. I was like, whatever."
—Simone Biles

Carlotta apologized, and the head of the Italian Gymnastics Federation tweeted an apology on behalf of his gymnast, too, but rather than easing any tension, his words exposed his own racist beliefs. He said that the comment was referring to how the new scoring system's focus on difficulty favored people of color, who were "known to be more powerful," while discriminating against "typical Eastern European elegance." In effect, he was suggesting that Simone's win at the 2013 world championships and Gabby Douglas's win at the 2012 Olympic Games were because the scoring system gave black gymnasts an advantage while discriminating against white gymnasts. A quick look at the history of gymnastics shows that, far from being discriminated against, white gymnasts have dominated the sport since it first became part of the Olympic Games in 1928. As Ronald put it, "Normally it's not in her favor being black, at least not in the world that I live in."

Breaking Barriers

To say that the gymnastics rules favored athletes of color is wrong on many levels. Not only does it suggest that black people are in some way genetically predisposed to be more muscular and powerful than white athletes—a racist view that plagues many athletic events—but it also ignores the history of gymnastics.

When American women began to compete in sports at the turn of the century, many of these new athletic activities were available only to white women. They took place in country clubs and colleges, which most women of color did not have access to, either because of racist rules or because those places were too expensive. In many states, racist laws made it illegal for black people to use public sports facilities such as tennis courts and swimming pools. Black people breaking these laws could face violence and prosecution.

In 1980, Luci Collins was the first black gymnast to make the US Olympic team. Sadly, she never got to compete, as the US refused to take part in the Moscow Olympic Games for political reasons. In 1992, Dominique Dawes became the first black American woman to compete in artistic gymnastics at the Olympics. Dominique won bronze on floor and team gold. Pioneers such as Luci Collins, Dominique Dawes, and Gabby Douglas have inspired more black athletes to take up gymnastics.

DISTRACTIONS AND DEPARTURES

Simone didn't let the media storm distract her—she had bigger problems. After the world championships, Simone had surgery to remove a painful bone spur on her ankle caused by her hard landing at the US Classic in Chicago. The surgery wasn't dangerous, but Simone wasn't allowed to train for three weeks.

Once she was back in the gym, Simone injured her shoulder. Again, it wasn't serious, but she needed physical therapy and rest if she was going to get better. Simone wasn't allowed to compete, but she could still train as long as she steered clear of the bars.

As well as battling injury, in February 2014, Simone faced further disruption. Aimee had fallen out with the owners of the gym and didn't want to work there anymore. One day during practice, she stormed out of Bannon's. Aimee had been Simone's coach since she was seven years old, and although Simone had worked with other coaches at Bannon's, Aimee was the one person who had been by her side from the very beginning.

Simone wasn't sure what to do without her coach. Nellie spoke to Aimee and told her that wherever she went, they'd go too. If that meant building their own gym, that's exactly what they would do.

Nellie began looking around for a suitable site. If she sold the nursing homes, they would be able to afford the land they would need to build a gym where Simone could train. They would also be able to run the gym as a business, offering lessons to other young gymnasts. In the interim, Nellie rented space for Aimee and Simone in another gym, but it was hard fitting their sessions around the gym's already busy schedule. They decided to rent a nearby warehouse instead. Nellie hired more coaches, and gymnasts soon began to join. It may only have been a warehouse, but how many warehouses could boast a world champion as a student?

⇂ THE WINNING STREAK ⇃

Once her shoulder healed, Simone's 2014 season went even better than 2013. She won gold in the all-around US Classic in Chicago, the competition Aimee had pulled her from the previous year, as well as gold on vault, beam, and floor. In August of that year, she won gold in the all-around at the US Gymnastics Championships for the second year running, and took gold on vault and floor.

In Nanning, China, Simone became the world champion in the all-around competition for the second year in a row, but it was her performance on the podium that went viral. Simone noticed a bee in her bouquet and freaked out! Unable to shake the bee out of the flowers, Simone screamed and hopped off the podium to escape, dropping her flowers onto the floor! Eventually, the bee transferred its attention to the bouquet of bronze medalist Kyla Ross, who left it on her podium and joined a laughing Simone for photographs on the top step.

WORLD CHAMPIONS CENTRE

Nellie and Ron were doing everything they could to get their new business venture off the ground. It was tougher than they expected, but in 2014 Simone was able to move out of the warehouse and start training in her very own gym, though it wouldn't officially open for another year. Compared to the dark warehouse, the gym was light and airy, and the space was much bigger. They decided to call it World Champions Centre.

CAN YOU THREE-PEAT THE QUESTION?

In almost every interview Simone gave in 2015, she was asked the same question: Could she "three-peat" and become world champion in the all-around competition for the third year in a row? The pressure was immense. She had won gold in every single all-around competition she had taken part in since the US Gymnastics Championships in 2013, and she was showing no signs of letting up. If anything, Simone was getting stronger, and her routines were getting more difficult. She was always pushing herself to try new things.

However, Simone's all-around performance at the 2015 world championships in Glasgow, Scotland, wasn't her best. She narrowly avoided falling off the beam and landed out of bounds during her floor routine. But the difficulty of her routines saved her: Simone won gold in the individual all-around by more than one point and became the first woman to win three consecutive world championships. Simone was happy to have won—and happy not to hear any more about whether or not she would do the "three-peat."

Simone had almost everything a gymnast could want. She had three world championships under her belt and her own world-class training facility. She was a three-time national champion and a hot favorite for a spot on the 2016 women's artistic gymnastics Olympic team. All her success hadn't gone unnoticed. Simone was approached by sponsors, companies wanting her to endorse their products in return for payment in the run-up to the Olympic Games.

If Simone was going to turn pro, now was the time to do it. But she still hoped to go to college and had accepted a scholarship offer from her dream school, the University of California, Los Angeles (UCLA). Simone didn't know what to do. If she took a sponsorship deal, she would have to give up the idea of college gymnastics, but if she took the scholarship, she would potentially miss out on all the good things that come with professional athletics.

It was a tough decision, but in July 2015, Simone made the choice to go pro. She had her sights set on a dream that few gymnasts get close to achieving: Olympic gold.

CHAPTER 6

THE FINAL FIVE

Simone had always written down her goals at the start of each year, but at the beginning of 2016, she found she didn't want to. Simone's goal for the year was to be selected as one of the five members of the US gymnastics team traveling to the Olympics. She wanted to win, of course, but she was also eager just to experience staying in the Olympic Village and meeting famous athletes from around the world. This had been her aim for five years, ever since she realized she would be too young to compete in the 2012 games. Now that she was so close, Simone worried it might not happen.

2016 GOALS

1. Make the US Olympic team.
2. Make the US Olympic team.
3. Make the US Olympic team.
4. Make the US Olympic team.

⋛ MAKING THE TEAM ⋚

Everyone told Simone she was certain to make the team.
The press went even further, predicting that she was the
country's best hope of bringing home five gold medals.
But nothing was certain. Even though Simone had won
every all-around competition she had entered since
2013, and was performing skills in competitions that few
gymnasts would even attempt in practice, she still had to
qualify at the team trials.

The trials took place in July 2016 in San José,
California, just one month before the team was due to
fly out to Rio. The previous national team trials that
Simone had taken part in had been held at the ranch,
where she'd performed in front of only a few people.
The SAP Stadium in San José held an audience of
nearly twenty thousand, and it was sold out. Perhaps
because of the big crowd or the pressure, Simone and
some of the other gymnasts did not perform at their
best. Simone took a huge step forward on the landing
of her Amanar vault and wobbled dangerously during
her wolf turn. On the second night, she fell off the
beam while trying to land her front flip with a half
twist. Olympic champion Gabby Douglas, a favorite

to make the team a second time, fell not once but twice on the beam.

The only guaranteed spot on the Olympic team went to the winner of the all-around competition. In spite of her errors, Simone made the top spot. She was going to Rio, but who would be going with her?

After all the gymnasts had competed, the selection committee, including Márta, discussed the results and chose their team. The energy in the stadium was electric as the names of the 2016 team were read out. Red, white, and blue confetti rained down from the ceiling as the athletes hugged each other and cried.

2016 US Women's Gymnastics Team

- Simone Biles
- Gabby Douglas
- Laurie Hernandez
- Madison Kocian
- Aly Raisman

It's a moment I'll feel forever.... I'm excited about the whole team being together to start training.

There was a tradition for the women's artistic gymnastics team to give themselves a name. The 2012 Olympic team had called themselves the Fierce Five. Simone and the other girls agreed on the Final Five, both in honor of the fact that they would be the last team coached by Márta Károlyi, who had announced that she would retire after the games, and because they would be the last team of five to compete. The plan was that for the 2020 Olympic Games onward, teams for women's gymnastics would shrink to four, but starting in 2024, teams will have five gymnasts again.

The Final Five

Along with Simone Biles, these gymnasts made up the Final Five:

GABBY DOUGLAS (See page 72.)

LAURIE HERNANDEZ
Born: June 9, 2000
At 16 years old, Laurie was the youngest member of the Final Five. The 2016 Olympics was her first major international competition.
Star events: balance beam and an expressive floor routine

MADISON KOCIAN

Born: June 15, 1997

Madison won gold at the 2015 national championships on uneven bars and tied for first at the world championships in the same event. Madison was specially selected for the Olympics to give the team the best chance at achieving a medal in this event.

Star event: uneven bars

ALY RAISMAN (See page 73.)

Simone had qualified for the team in first place, but a stumble on beam showed she still had work to do if she wanted to be sure of gold. She would have to improve quickly—they were due to fly to Rio in just sixteen days.

≍ THE PRESSURE ≍

Training got off to a bad start. When Simone returned to the World Champions Centre after the trials, she kept messing up her routines and getting angry with herself. Aimee had to send her home. The pressure was too much for Simone to handle. Every magazine seemed to carry a story about how she was going to win gold—but how could she do that when she couldn't even manage the routines at her own gym? When asked how she was handling the pressure, Simone replied,

BILES EXPECTED TO DOMINATE IN RIO OLYMPICS

Rio 201

"I feel like it's harder because everyone knows I'm the three-time world champion—it's almost like people are waiting for something bad to happen. . . . That kind of stresses me out a bit."

A call to her therapist, Robert, set her straight. Once again, he reminded her that she had no control over other people's expectations. All she could do was relax, have fun, and be the best Simone she could be.

⋛ TEAM TRAINING ⋚

Before the team members traveled to Rio, they were invited to attend a final ten-day training camp at the Károlyi Ranch. It would be their last chance to iron out any kinks in their routines before the games.

They then flew from Houston to Rio on Tuesday, July 26. The girls tried to sleep on the plane but kept getting disturbed by passengers who wanted to take selfies with them! When they arrived at the Olympic Village, they checked in at the welcome center before taking their things to their third-floor apartment in the USA building.

Olympic Village, Rio

During the Olympic Games, all athletes stay in the Olympic Village. In Rio, 31 towers, each 17 stories tall, were built to house the athletes for the duration of the competition. Team USA had a whole tower to itself, but countries with fewer competitors shared buildings, occupying different floors. The towers contained separate apartments, each with bedrooms, a common area, and a balcony.

Around the towers, the athletes could socialize on a human-made beach, swim in one of several outdoor pools, or play a match on the tennis courts. There was a 24-hour cafeteria that served food from all over the world, along with shops and even a McDonald's restaurant.

OLYMPIC ATHLETE PASS

NAME: SIMONE BILES

GYMNASTICS

⌇ TOP TEAM ⌇

On August 7, Simone's team got its first chance
to show what it could do at the Olympic qualifier
competition. In the qualifier, gymnasts compete to
decide who will take part in the finals in each event. The
twenty-four highest-scoring gymnasts across all of
the events, with a maximum of two per national team,
progress to the individual all-around competition final.
The eight gymnasts who achieve the highest scores on
each piece of apparatus, with a maximum of two per
national team, progress to the individual event finals,
and the eight teams with the highest combined scores
go on to compete in the team final.

Simone, Aly, and Gabby placed first, second, and
third, respectively. All of them scored high enough
to qualify for the all-around competition final, but
Olympic rules meant that only the top two could
compete. As well as the all-around competition,
Simone qualified in first place for beam, vault, and
floor. Gabby and Madison qualified to compete in
uneven bars, Laurie on beam, and Aly on floor. Simone
and her teammates qualified in first place for the team
competition, which would take place two days later.

In between competing and training, the girls had the chance to explore the village and swap selfies with other sports celebrities, such as US swimmer Michael Phelps and UK diver Tom Daley.

The gymnastics teams stood out because they weren't as tall as the athletes competing in many of the other sports. At their apartment, the girls watched Netflix on Simone's computer, listened to music, and took naps. Aly Raisman—the eldest member of the team, nicknamed "Grandma" by the other girls— napped the most.

But the team didn't have too much time to relax. On August 9, two days after the Olympic qualifier, the Final Five returned to the arena for the team competition. They put in a slick performance and won gold.

READY TO WIN

On August 11, Simone and Aly got ready for the individual all-around competition. Simone put on her favorite leotard—it was glossy red, white, and blue, sprinkled with shimmering stars. In the training hall, Simone and Aly warmed up by practicing their routines, performing them almost flawlessly. There was nothing more they could do.

The first event was the vault. Simone sprinted down the runway and pushed off the table, spinning twice in the air, followed by a half twist, before landing on the mat with just a small step to steady herself. Her Amanar wasn't perfect—the step on landing cost her a small deduction—but she received maximum points for difficulty. Her score of 15.866 flashed up on the screen, putting her in first place.

The second event was Simone's least favorite: the uneven bars. Simone's routine was a lower difficulty level than some of the other competitors', but with good execution, she still hoped to get a high score. As Simone mounted the low bar and began her routine, she heard Nellie shout out from the crowd:

Simone felt she flew higher on her releases than she had ever done before, catching the bar and swinging into the next element with ease. Simone prepared to dismount, swinging faster and faster, before releasing the bar and taking off into the air. She beamed as her feet landed on the mat without so much as a hop. The bar routine had gone well, but her score wasn't as high as she had hoped. For the first time since 2013, Simone's name appeared lower on an all-around competition scoreboard than another competitor, Russian gymnast Aliya Mustafina.

Next up in the rotation was beam. Simone knew if she could complete all the difficult elements of her routine, she would still be in the running for gold. From the two and a half spins of her wolf turn to her dismount, considered to be one of the most difficult in the world, it was clear she was in the zone.

She smiled broadly at the judges after performing a full-twisting double tuck, a maneuver many gymnasts would have a hard time completing on the floor, never mind on the four-inch-wide beam. The judges' score of 15.433 was more than enough to put her safely in the lead. Aly's beam routine had been solid, although she hopped on the landing, but Simone's routines had such a high degree of difficulty that unless she really messed up on floor, she was sure of gold before the first beats of her music even began.

A gymnast's floor routine is her chance to show her personality, and Simone's personality filled the arena. When the scores were revealed, Simone took gold, winning by more than two points, while Aly took silver.

Simone didn't normally cry after a competition, but this wasn't just any competition; it was the Olympic Games, and Simone could not contain her emotions. Winning Olympic gold meant the world to Simone. It had been her dream to compete ever since she was a little girl. In an interview with CNN following the event, Simone said, "It's like everything that has led me up to this moment has paid off and has all been worth it. I have no regrets."

EVENT FINALS

Simone may have already won two Olympic gold medals, but there were more events to come in the days that followed. On August 14, Simone won the vault competition and became the first American woman to bring home gold in that event. On August 15, she took bronze on beam, and on August 16, Simone made it three medals in three days by taking gold on floor.

The rest of the team did well, too. Laurie won silver on beam, Aly silver on floor, and Madison silver on uneven bars. The Final Five won nine medals between them, making them the most decorated US gymnastics team in history.

⋝ LEADING THE FIELD ⋜

For Simone, the days after the Olympics were a blur. Everybody wanted to talk to her, including her celebrity crush, Zac Efron, who had flown all the way to Rio to surprise her live on television! Tributes from celebrities flooded in, including a message from President Barack Obama.

Simone's Olympic experience got even better when the rest of Team USA nominated her to carry the flag at the closing ceremony.

The nine-foot flagpole was almost twice as tall as she was—Simone worried she might drop it, especially when the night of the closing ceremony turned out to be a windy one! But her nerves soon settled when she realized that if she could use her strength and determination to win five medals, carrying a flag should be no problem. As she walked into the stadium followed by the rest of the team, she knew she had made her country, her family, and, most important, herself proud.

CHAPTER 7

THE NEXT ROTATION

Simone had achieved her number one goal, the goal she had been too scared to write down at the beginning of 2016. She decided she was going to take a break from gymnastics and spend some time doing all the things her busy schedule had prevented her from doing. Growing up in the sport, Simone had been forced to say no to a lot of activities because there was a risk she could get injured, or simply because she was too busy training and traveling. Simone wanted the year after the Olympics to be the year she got to say:

YES!

A YEAR OF SAYING YES

One of the first things Simone said yes to was a trip away. Simone had missed out on family vacations because she had to be available to travel to all the training camps, competitions, and qualifiers. After the Olympics, Simone had the time, and the money from her sponsorship deals, to travel the world. Two of the places Simone visited with her family were Belize and Hawaii.

Simone said yes to extreme sports, too. While she was training, Simone had avoided activities that could lead to injury, to keep herself in peak physical condition for competition.

Splash!

Hawaii, 2017

After the Olympics, Simone tried cliff jumping, horseback riding, and indoor skydiving.

Having turned down her chance to attend UCLA on a gymnastics scholarship, Simone had also missed out on going to college. She enrolled in University of the People, an online higher-education institution, and began working toward a degree in business administration.

Simone hadn't gone to high school; she'd never gone to any school dances or to prom. She took part in season twenty-four of *Dancing with the Stars*, alongside her dance partner, Sasha Farber. Simone showed just what a fierce competitor she is and placed fourth. During one episode, she put the

Let's fox-trot!

host, Tom Bergeron, firmly in his place when he asked why she didn't smile more for the judges. "Smiling doesn't win you gold medals," she told him.

BACK TO THE MAT

In August 2017, Simone returned to training and started practicing again at the World Champions Centre. At first she took it easy to see how her body had changed after her time off. Following the first few sessions, Simone was in so much pain that she couldn't sleep and could barely walk up and down the stairs, never mind pull off one of her signature moves!

"There are some things I look back at and am like, 'I have to do that again?' It wasn't scary before, but it's scary now."
—Simone Biles

But Simone pushed through, and by November 1, 2017, she was back on a training schedule similar to the one she had followed before the Olympics.

Simone's Daily Schedule

7:00 a.m.	Wake-up
8:00 a.m.	Breakfast of cereal or egg whites
9:00 a.m.	Three-hour training session at the gym
Noon	High-protein lunch, usually including chicken or fish
1:00 p.m.	School or therapy
2:00 p.m.	Protein snack
3:00 p.m.	Three-hour training session
6:00 p.m.	Physical therapy at home or at the gym
7:00 p.m.	Dinner with family
8:00 p.m.	Relaxation/catch-up with friends and family
9:00 p.m.	College work
11:00 p.m.	Bed

⋜ SAYING GOODBYE ⋝

After Rio, Simone said goodbye to her longtime coach Aimee Boorman. Aimee had moved to Florida with her family and found work at another gym. Aimee had been by Simone's side as her coach since Simone was seven years old. When Aimee had left Bannon's, Simone had followed her. Even though she didn't want to say goodbye, Simone couldn't follow her this time. Now Simone and her family owned their own gym, and Simone was the face of the whole business and the reason many gymnasts chose to train there.

Simone needed a new coach. She chose a man named Laurent Landi, who had previously coached Simone's Final Five teammate Madison for the 2016 Olympics. Madison was selected for the 2016 Olympic team because of her excellent uneven-bar work. Simone hoped Laurent would help her improve her performance on her least favorite apparatus.

Laurent Landi

Laurent Landi was born in France in 1977. Laurent was a member of the French national gymnastics team and won bronze on the high bar at the Junior European Championships in 1994. In 1999, Laurent began coaching at the club where he had trained in Antibes, France. Three years later, Laurent moved to Marseille to work with the French national team before moving to the US in 2004.

In 2007, Laurent started working at the World Olympic Gymnastics Academy in Texas, where he coached world champion Alyssa Baumann and 2016 Olympic gold and silver medalist Madison Kocian. In 2017, Laurent became the girls team program director at World Champions Centre, the gym owned by Ronald and Nellie Biles, and took over as Simone's head coach.

⋛ SIMONE SPEAKS OUT ⋛

As Simone built up her strength in the gym, USA Gymnastics was falling apart. It had been discovered that Larry Nassar, one of the on-site doctors at the Károlyi Ranch, had sexually abused many of the young gymnasts who were supposed to be under his care. On January 24, 2018, the disgraced doctor was sentenced to a minimum of forty years in prison for his crimes.

After the trial, Simone added her voice to those of the 265 women and girls who came forward as having been abused. "Most of you know me as a happy, giggly, and energetic girl," she wrote in a statement that she shared on Twitter. "But lately I've felt a bit broken, and the more I try to shut off the voice in my head, the louder it screams. I am not afraid to tell my story anymore. I, too, am one of the many survivors that was sexually abused by Larry Nassar. . . . There are many reasons that I have been reluctant to share my story, but I know now it is not my fault." Simone, like the other victims, handled the situation with great bravery. She wouldn't let the horrible things that had happened to her stop her from achieving her dreams.

Following Larry Nassar's conviction, many believed

that the people in charge at USAG were also to blame and should have listened to the gymnasts sooner. The US Olympic Committee called for everyone working on the board at USAG to resign. Not long after, USA Gymnastics released a statement that it would no longer be holding training camps at the Károlyi Ranch.

At the end of January 2018, Simone appeared on the *Today* show to talk about coming to terms with what had happened to her. She had a message for fellow survivors of similar abuse that it is not their fault.

SIMONE SPEAKS OUT

Inappropriate Touch

It is not acceptable for someone to touch a child's body in a way that makes the child uncomfortable. That is inappropriate touch. If someone touches a child's private parts, this is called child sexual abuse. Children should not be afraid to say no to any kind of touching that makes them feel bad, even if they know the person doing it.

If a doctor needs to examine a child's private parts, it should be quick, and another adult, such as a parent, guardian, or nurse, should be in the room. The doctor should also explain what is happening.

Sexual abuse is a crime. If you are worried that you have been, or are being, abused, or you feel like someone has touched you or behaved in a way that makes you uncomfortable, do not keep it a secret. Speak to an adult you trust. It is important to remember that you have done nothing wrong.

⋛ BACK ON FORM ⋚

Many wondered if Simone, after a year away from training, would be able to compete at the level she had previously. Simone tried to shut out the pressure. Once she was back in the gym and into a routine, she started to increase the difficulty of the moves she attempted during practice, listening to both her coaches and her own body. In March, USAG announced that Simone was back on the national team.

At the 2018 national championships in Boston, Simone became the first woman to win gold in all five events: the all-around competition, vault, balance beam, floor, and what had always been her weakest event, uneven bars. It seemed that Simone was not only back, but better than ever.

During the 2018 world championships in Doha, Qatar, Simone felt severe pain in her back. She was admitted to the hospital and diagnosed with kidney stones. Simone postponed treatment and fought through the pain in order to compete, tweeting:

 Simone Biles
@simone_biles

Nothing like a late-night ER visit less than 24 hours before world championships. This kidney stone can wait . . . doing it for my team!

Her performance wasn't perfect. . . .
She sat down on the landing of her vault.

She wobbled and fell off the beam.

She stepped out of bounds on her floor routine.

But she still won gold! Simone may have dropped points on execution, but the difficulty of her routines meant she won the individual all-around competition by a margin of 1.693. Over the course of the competition, Simone also took gold on vault and floor, silver on uneven bars, and bronze on balance beam.

Simone took home four gold medals and became the first female gymnast to win gold in the individual all-around competition in four world championships. Simone was disappointed in her performance, however, and felt she could have done better. "It's not the gymnast that I am," she said. "To go out there and kind of bomb a meet like this. Even though I won, I wish it were a little bit different." After the competition, Simone got treatment for the kidney stones and took a well-earned vacation.

NEW CONFIDENCE

At the US Classic in July 2019, Simone embraced the fact that she was in a class of her own, wearing a personalized leotard with *BILES* spelled out in rhinestones on the back. Simone showed that this confidence wasn't just for the practice session by winning her fourth gold in the all-around competition by more than two points. Some critics thought Simone was vain to wear a leotard with her own name on it, but she disagreed. She thought it was important for gymnasts to take pride in their achievements.

In fact, Simone hinted that it was more than just her leotard she wanted her name on. Simone already had two skills named after her in the *Code of Points*, one on floor and one on vault, but at the US Classic she showed that she was ready for more. In practice Simone performed a triple-twisting double flip, which was a skill so difficult, no woman had ever performed it in competition before. Though she left it out of her program, Simone demonstrated that she was capable of performing it and that it was only a matter of time before she added to her routines.

> You'll go your whole entire career and everybody will tell you you're great. But the minute you say you're good, [people are] like, "Oh my gosh, you're so cocky!"

SOMEONE GIVE THIS GIRL A CROWN

At the national championships in August 2019, Simone attended practice in a leotard that had not only her name on the back but also the glittering face of a goat—*GOAT* is the acronym for "greatest of all time." It was her way of getting back at her critics without even saying a word. Her history-making gymnastics during that competition left commentators struggling to come up with new words to describe performances unlike anything the sport had seen before.

"Simone's got enough gold medals at home; someone give this girl a crown."
—Nastia Liukin, commentator

MAKING HISTORY

In August 2019, Simone became the first woman in sixty-seven years to win gold in the individual all-around competition in six national championships. Simone also became the first woman to perform not one but two brand-new moves, proving without doubt she is the greatest gymnast of all time.

SIMONE
BILES

Simone's
History-Making Moves

On Beam

Simone was the first gymnast to
successfully perform a double-twisting,
double-flip dismount on beam. The move is
so difficult, many world-class gymnasts
are unable to perform it on the floor,
never mind on a four-inch-wide beam.

On Floor

Simone became the first female gymnast
to execute the hardest move performed on
the floor exercise: the triple-double.
The move consists of a back handspring
followed by two flips and three twists

in tucked position. It is considered so difficult that only a few male artistic gymnasts have performed it in competition, and none performed it at the 2019 national championships. Tom Forster, the man in charge of selecting the 2020 US Olympic team, said he believes a new difficulty category should be created for it.

≥ MIC DROP AT WORLDS ≤

Performing these moves at an international competition would mean they would be named after her in the FIG *Code of Points*. Thankfully, Simone wouldn't have long to wait.

In October, Simone traveled to Stuttgart, Germany, to compete in the 2019 Artistic Gymnastics World Championships. She won gold medals in the team competition, the event finals for vault, beam, and floor and her fifth gold medal in the individual all-around competition.

Simone's win brought her world championship medal total to twenty-five, making her the most decorated gymnast in history, male or female, beating the twenty-three-medal record set by Belarusian male gymnast Vitaly Scherbo.

In addition to her history-making medal win, Simone debuted her double-twisting, double-flip dismount on beam and her triple-twisting double flip on floor. So now the new skills bear her name in the gymnastics *Code of Points*.

Simone completed her record-breaking floor routine in the individual all-around final by dropping an imaginary microphone, showing she is fully aware of her athletic greatness. Afterward, she told *USA Today,* "It's important to teach our female youth that it's okay to say, 'Yes, I am good at this.'"

⋛ READY TO WIN ⋚

Growing up, Simone had worried she would be too old to compete in the 2016 Olympics, let alone the Tokyo Games in 2020. After her performance at the world championships, it is clear that far from being too old, Simone is performing at a higher level than she (or any other gymnast) has performed at before.

CONCLUSION

MAKING HISTORY

When Simone Biles tumbles across the floor or flies off the vault and lands with a smile, she makes gymnastics look effortless. It would be easy to forget how impressive her achievements really are. Simone has won so many medals and broken so many records that the fact that she is the greatest gymnast of all time is no longer up for debate. Even Simone has embraced the title.

When Simone competes, she doesn't just win— she wins by huge margins. At the 2019 national championships, she won by almost five full points.

"Every day in training
I amaze myself even more."
—Simone Biles

With each competition, Simone is changing the sport of gymnastics forever, making people rethink what is possible for an athlete to achieve. Since the 2019 Artistic Gymnastics World Championships, Simone has four moves named after her in the FIG *Code of Points:* two on floor, one on vault, and one on balance beam. Olympic individual all-around gold medalist and commentator Nastia Liukin said of Simone's performance at the 2019 national championships, "A few years ago, I feel like if someone would have told me that anybody would be doing this skill, even in training . . . I wouldn't have believed them."

Many sports commentators have compared Simone to other great athletes, but Simone doesn't let that pressure get to her.

I'm not the next Usain Bolt or Michael Phelps. I'm the first Simone Biles.

Simone's Greatest Hits

During her relatively short career, Simone has broken many records. Here are a few of her greatest achievements:

- Simone has won gold in every individual all-around competition she has entered since the US Gymnastics Championships in 2013.

- Simone is a six-time national champion in the all-around competition.

- Simone is a five-time world champion in the all-around competition.

- Simone won gold in the 2016 Rio Olympics all-around competition and took home gold on vault and floor, as well as team gold and bronze on beam.

- Simone has won more world championship medals than any gymnast in history.

Books and Movies

Simone's success at the Olympic Games and world championships has made her a household name. People all over the world want to know more about her and discover how she became so successful. Simone has appeared on the cover of magazines, including *Teen Vogue, Ebony, Glamour,* and *Time*.

Simone shared her own life story in her autobiography, *Courage to Soar: A Body in Motion, A Life in Balance*, which was published in November 2016. The book became a number one bestseller.

Not long after Simone's book came out, the Lifetime TV channel started work on a movie based on her story. The film premiered on February 3, 2018.

Power Gymnast

Simone is known for being a powerful gymnast—able to jump higher, spin faster, and leap farther than anyone else in her sport—but Simone's voice has power, too. With over one million followers on Twitter, Simone uses her platform to speak out about causes she believes in.

Simone continues to speak up for herself and fellow victims of convicted child abuser Larry Nassar. In August 2019, a US Senate panel concluded that Larry was enabled by USA Gymnastics and the US Olympic Committee (USOC). In response to the news, Simone called for more work to be done to protect athletes, tweeting, "The more I learn, the more I hurt. USAG failed us. USOC failed us. Many failed us. And they continue to fail us. Real and actual change isn't easy, but it's clear there's a lot more work that needs to be done."

SIMONE BILES LEGACY SCHOLARSHIP FUND

Although Simone was very young when she lived with a foster family, she remembers how tough it was. She wanted to do something to help other children in foster care, by giving them an opportunity to attend college.

Only 50 percent of young adults who have been through the foster care system graduate from high school, and only one in five of those goes on to higher education. To help change that, Simone set up the Simone Biles Legacy Scholarship Fund to cover the cost of tuition for young people in foster care. Simone also teamed up with a Houston-based mattress company to further help children in foster care across the United States. As a spokesperson for the program, Simone encourages people around the country to donate items such as books, clothes, and soft toys. The mattress company distributes these items to children going into care to help them settle into their new homes.

⋛ BILES STYLE ⋚

In November 2015, Simone Biles announced that she had become a brand ambassador for a company called GK Elite Sportswear. Simone was given the opportunity to make one of her dreams come true— to design her own range of leotards. Thanks to this deal, gymnasts can train and compete in leotards designed by their favorite world champion and can even purchase replicas of some of the leotards Simone has worn in competition.

$\equiv$ SIMONE BILES DAY $\equiv$

On November 27, 2018, Simone and her mother, Nellie, were invited to attend a ceremony at City Hall in Houston, Texas. At the ceremony, Mayor Sylvester Turner presented Simone with a framed proclamation and a key to the city. The proclamation reads that Houston recognizes "outstanding individuals who hone their dedication and prowess to break barriers and serve as inspiration to others." As well as honoring Simone, the mayor and city council members paid tribute to Simone's family, saying that their support and commitment to Simone made the Bileses a "family of champions." In recognition of Simone becoming the most decorated female gymnast in the history of world championships, November 27 was declared Simone Biles Day.

HAPPY SIMONE BILES DAY!

⋛ SIMONE INSPIRES ⋜

Simone is an inspiration to people all over the world. Every time she pushes the boundaries of her abilities by adding an extra twist or flip to her routine, she challenges other athletes to push themselves further, too. Simone hopes that when young athletes see her standing on the podium, they think, "If she can do it, I can do it."

But Simone isn't just an inspiration to athletes; she is an inspiration to everyone. Simone is a symbol of what a person can achieve with hard work and dedication. Simone did not have the easiest start in life. She survived sexual abuse and bore the brunt of racist comments throughout her career. As Simone worked tirelessly, made sacrifices, and battled injury, her family—Ronald and Nellie Biles, Adria, Adam, and Ron Jr.—were making sacrifices and battling alongside her, clearing the way so that she could achieve her dreams.

⋛ SIMONE 2020 ⋚

In 2020, Simone hopes to travel to Tokyo to compete as a member of the USA women's gymnastics team. The selection process for the 2020 team promises to be even tougher than that for the 2016 team, with the number of athletes allowed to compete reduced from five to four. Two extra spots are available for event specialists, but these gymnasts are not allowed to take part in the team competition, and even have to wear different leotards.

The team for the Tokyo Olympics will be announced following a training camp and selection competition in June 2020. If Simone avoids injury and continues to perform at the level seen in 2019, she is not only guaranteed to make the team but very likely to make history once again.

Timeline

March 14
Simone Biles is born in Columbus, OH.

Simone visits Bannon's Gymnastix on a day care field trip and start lessons at the gym soon after

1997   2000   2003

Simone and her siblings—Tevin, Ashley, and Adria—are taken into foster care.

November
Simone and Adr: are officially adopted by Ronald and Nellie Biles.

August 15
Simone competes in her first US Gymnastics Championships in Hartford, CT. Simone wins a gold medal in the individual all-around competition and silver medals in each of the other events.

2013

October 4
Simone competes in her first World Artistic Gymnastics Championships in Antwerp, Belgium. She wins a gold medal in the individual all-around competition and floor exercise, a silver on vault, and a bronze on balance beam. Following the championships, a move Simone performed during her floor routine is added to the FIG *Code of Points*.

June 10
Simone is selected as a member of the US Junior National Team after placing third in the individual all-round competition at the 2012 US Gymnastics Championships in St. Louis, MO.

2012

2013

July/August
At the 2012 Olympic Games in London, the US women's gymnastics team—the Fierce Five—wins gold in the team competition.

July 27
Simone takes part in the 2013 US Classic in Chicago, IL. Simone gives a disastrous performance and is pulled from competition by coach Aimee Boorman.

May
World Champions Centre, the world-class training facility owned by Ronald and Nellie Biles, opens to the public.

2014

2015

February
mee Boorman leaves Bannon's Gymnastix.

October 29
Simone becomes the first woman to win a gold medal in the individual all-around competition at three consecutive World Artistic Gymnastics Championships.

August 6—21

Simone Biles wins five medals at the 2016 Summer Olympic Games in Rio, Brazil. She achieves gold medals in the individual all-around competition, team competition, vault, and floor exercise, as well as a bronze medal on balance beam.

2016

Simone Biles's life story, *Courage to Soar*, is published and soon becomes a *New York Times* bestseller.

August 19

Simone wins a gold medal in every event at the US Gymnastics Championships in Boston, MA.

2018

November 3

Simone becomes the first American woman to win a medal in every event at the World Artistic Gymnastics Championships, taking gold medals in the team, individual all-around, vault, and floor exercise, as well as silver on uneven bars and bronze on balance beam.

February 3
The movie *The Simone Biles Story: Courage to Soar* premieres on the Lifetime television network.

2017

2018

March 20
Simone Biles takes part in the twenty-fourth season of *Dancing with the Stars*.

October
Simone wins five gold medals at the 2019 World Artistic Gymnastics Championships in Stuttgart, Germany, making her the most decorated gymnast of all time.

2019

December 21
"The Biles"—the vault first performed by Simone at the 2018 world championships—is added to the FIG *Code of Points*.

Further Reading

→ *Courage to Soar: A Body in Motion, A Life in Balance* by Simone Biles with Michelle Burford (Zondervan, 2016)

→ *Gymnastics: A Guide for Athletes and Fans* (Sport Zone) by Matt Chandler (Capstone Press, 2019)

→ *Simone Biles: Gymnastics Star* by Lori Mortenson (Capstone Press, 2018)

→ *Sports All-Stars: Simone Biles* by Jon M. Fishman (Lerner Publications, 2017)

Websites

→ olympic.org

The official website of the Olympic Games, including information on past and future events.

→ simonebiles.com

The official website of Simone Biles, including latest news.

Glossary

addiction: A powerful and destructive need to regularly consume a substance such as alcohol or other habit-forming drugs.

adoption: The legal process by which the parental rights and responsibilities for a child are permanently transferred to someone other than the child's biological parents.

amateur: A person who takes part in an activity as a pastime or hobby rather than a profession.

apparatus: A set of equipment, such as the beam, vault, or bars, used in gymnastics competitions.

cartwheel: An acrobatic move in which a person travels sideways in a full circle from a standing position, landing first on the hands and then on the feet.

Glossary

diagnosed: Recognized to have a disease or medical condition.

dormitory: A large room for sleeping, containing several beds.

elite (gymnastics): The most advanced level of gymnastics, in which the most difficult skills are performed.

foster care: Temporary care for children whose parents are unable to look after them.

homeschool: To teach a student at home instead of sending them to a school.

incentive: Something that motivates or encourages a person to act.

<u>Glossary</u>

leotard: A formfitting item of clothing often worn for gymnastics and dance.

psychologist: A person who specializes in studying people's behavior and treats conditions related to the mind.

rhinestone: A shiny stone or piece of glass or plastic cut to sparkle like a diamond, sometimes used to decorate clothing.

scholarship: An amount of money awarded to a student by a college or an organization to help fund the student's education.

social worker: A professional who works with individuals, families, and communities to improve their well-being in areas of financial stability; access to food, housing, or health care; and physical safety and welfare at home.

Glossary

stamina: The strength (physical or mental) that helps a person continue to do something for a long time.

tumbling: Gymnastics moves (such as flips and handsprings) performed on the floor.

Index

Index

Index

Index

Index

FOLLOW THE TRAIL!

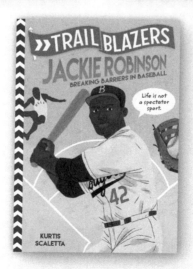

TURN THE PAGE FOR A SNEAK PEEK AT THESE TRAILBLAZERS BIOGRAPHIES!

TRAIL BLAZERS
STEPHEN HAWKING
A LIFE BEYOND LIMITS
We can understand the universe.
ALEX WOOLF

A Theory of Everything

Quantum mechanics explains how the world works at the scale of the very small, while Einstein's theory of general relativity explains how the world works on the scale of the large. The trouble is, they describe what seem like two different universes. At large scales, gravity is the dominant force; in the quantum world, three other forces—electromagnetism and the strong and weak nuclear forces—hold sway. The great challenge of physics over the past century has been to find a "theory of everything," a set of laws that describe how the universe works at all scales.

⋝ PRESENTING THE DISCOVERY ⋜

Stephen told his colleagues about his discovery in January 1974. It caused huge excitement. His friend Martin Rees told Dennis Sciama: "Have you heard? Stephen's changed everything!" Roger Penrose phoned Stephen, who was just sitting down to his birthday dinner with family and guests. Penrose was so excited, he kept Stephen talking for ages, and the food got cold.

Stephen formally presented his idea at a conference in Oxford in February. It was met with a baffled silence. Many in the audience didn't understand Stephen's arguments. Those who did were shocked. How could anything come out of a black hole? The conference chairman, Professor John Taylor, eventually spoke up.

Sorry, Stephen, but this is absolute rubbish.

A UNIVERSE WITH NO BOUNDARIES

Stephen's research into the very early universe led him to some startling conclusions. In 1983, he published a paper with American physicist James Hartle describing what they termed the "no-boundary proposal." In this, they suggested that there might be no boundary—that is, no beginning or ending—to the universe. This was not to say that Stephen had lost faith in the big bang theory. What he was arguing was that scientists' whole understanding of the big bang was mistaken. In their paper, Hawking and Hartle asked readers to imagine traveling backward in time toward the very beginning of the universe.

THIS WAY TO **THE BIG BANG!**

As we approach the singularity that gave rise to the big bang, they wrote, everything becomes extremely compressed. It becomes so compressed that the differences between space and time disappear. Time becomes like another dimension of space. This is, of course, impossible for us to imagine with our human brains. Time isn't normally something we can see or touch—it's just the flow of events.

But what happens in the extremely early universe is that space and time merge to form something called four-dimensional space (you can't picture this, so don't even try!). This four-dimensional space curves around to become a closed surface, like a ball. A ball is not infinite in size, yet it has no edge or boundary, so anyone traveling across the ball's surface might think it is infinite.

And this, according to Hawking and Hartle, is how we should try to imagine the universe: not infinite, yet with no boundaries—no beginning or end.

This journey is taking forever!

WELCOME TIME TRAVELERS

I sat there a long tim[e] but no one came.

This was a lighthearted test of his proposal in 1992 that time travel to the past is impossible. If people had shown up, it would have proved him wrong.

≡ "RETIREMENT" ≡

In September 2009, Stephen retired from his post as Lucasian Professor of Mathematics at Cambridge after thirty years in the role. This followed an age-old custom that Lucasian professors retire at sixty-seven. Stephen wasn't thinking about really retiring, because he was still fizzing with energy and ideas. For the rest of his life, he would continue to work and travel, lecturing about topics such as the colonization of other planets, the origin of life, black holes, and the theory of everything. The only big setback was that he was unable to operate his wheelchair independently after 2009, so he was forced to rely on others to push him.

⊒ HAWKING VERSUS HIGGS ⊑

In 1964, British physicist Peter Higgs predicted the existence of a particle, later called the Higgs boson, that was necessary to make sense of the generally accepted theory about how the universe works at the quantum scale. Essentially, the Higgs boson was needed to give other particles their mass. The trouble was, the particle was elusive, and perhaps even impossible to observe. In 1996, Stephen predicted that the Higgs boson would never be found. He and Peter Higgs publicly clashed on the issue at a dinner in Edinburgh in 2002.

In 2008, an opportunity finally arrived to observe the Higgs boson, with the opening of the Large Hadron Collider (LHC), a very powerful new particle accelerator at CERN.

TRAIL BLAZERS
BEYONCÉ
QUEEN OF THE SPOTLIGHT
Power means hard work.
EBONY
JOY
WILKINS

A NEW PARTNERSHIP

Jay-Z and Beyoncé released a single together, "'03 Bonnie and Clyde." On the track, Jay-Z sings, "All I need in this life of sin is me and my girlfriend," to which Beyoncé replies, "Down to ride till the very end, is me and my boyfriend." For some fans, this was confirmation enough that the two were dating.

But even with rumors swirling, Beyoncé and Jay-Z refused to confirm or deny that they were together. When asked about the nature of their relationship, Jay-Z told one reporter, "She's beautiful. Who wouldn't wish she was their girlfriend? Maybe one day."

<u>Bonnie and Clyde</u>

Jay-Z and Beyoncé's track was named after
two infamous criminals who traveled the
United States together in the 1930s.
Bonnie and Clyde led police on a chase
across the country, robbing several
businesses and murdering 13 people. The
two were finally tracked down by a Texas
Ranger in Bienville Parish, Louisiana,
where they were shot and killed.

Every part of the performance had to be exactly right, from the backup dancers to the lighting. Her outfit, a tight black bodysuit, took two hundred hours to put together. Due to the intense rehearsal schedule, Beyoncé lost weight, and the waist had to be taken in repeatedly to ensure a flattering fit.

The set began with an explosion of red-and-white flares and a giant white outline of Beyoncé above the stage. Then the singer emerged to perform "Love on Top." Later, Beyoncé was joined by Michelle and Kelly, who rose up through hidden trapdoors to sing a few of Destiny's Child's greatest hits to the 70,000-strong crowd. To wrap up the performance, Beyoncé turned down the tempo and ended on the emotionally charged "Halo."

The set went down in history. The *New York Times* declared that Beyoncé had "silenced her doubters," and the British newspaper the *Daily Telegraph* called it a "take-no-prisoners assault on the senses." Moments after she had finished, a power outage in the stadium caused a delay to the second half. For many, Bey's performance had literally overshadowed the game.

TRAIL BLAZERS
JACKIE ROBINSON
BREAKING BARRIERS IN BASEBALL
Life is not a spectator sport.
UCLA
B
42
KURTIS SCALETTA

Jackie at UCLA
1939–1941

→ **Football:** Jackie is called "the greatest ball carrier in the nation." In 1939, the Bruins go undefeated, though three games end in ties.

→ **Basketball:** Dazzling play by Jackie helps end a long losing streak by the Bruins but isn't enough to give them a winning season.

→ **Baseball:** Jackie once again plays short and gets a reputation for stealing bases but goes into a hitting slump he can't break out of.

→ **Track and Field:** Jackie sets a conference record and wins the NCAA title for the long jump.

→ **Combined:** Jackie is the first athlete at UCLA to "letter" in four sports—meaning he has significant playing time at the varsity level.

LOVE AND WAR

Jackie continued to shine in his second year at UCLA, but the football team and basketball team both had losing seasons. Something happened that was more important than sports or even his education. He met a student named Rachel Isum. Jackie was drawn to Rachel's intelligence and compassion.

At first, he later wrote, Jackie experienced a new kind of prejudice. Rachel Isum knew he was a star athlete and had seen him play. She was convinced he was cocky and full of himself. But as she got to know him, she learned Jackie had a serious mind and—more important—respected that she had one, too. After they'd known each other for a year, they were deeply in love.

No matter what happens, this relationship is going to be one of the most important parts of my life.

Jackie's appeal crossed color lines. Author Myron Uhlberg wrote of how his deaf father connected with Jackie because they were both out of place in the world. Bette Bao Lord wrote a fictionalized memoir called *In the Year of the Boar and Jackie Robinson*, about how Jackie's courage helped her overcome her own barriers as a Chinese immigrant. Anyone who had ever been told they didn't belong, or who stood out for their differences, felt a connection.

And some fans loved Jackie simply because he was an exciting player to watch. He would get on base, take a lead, and dare the pitcher to make a throw. He was always a threat to steal. He would steal third base with two outs. He would steal home! Some fans compared him to baseball's all-time greatest base runner, Ty Cobb. Jackie's fearlessness on the base path lifted the rest of the team. They hit better because the pitchers were rattled and infielders were distracted.

Memorabilia

- Buddy Johnson record "Did You See Jackie Robinson Hit That Ball?"

- Collectible cards

- Cover of *Time* magazine

- Jackie Robinson comic book

COMING SOON . . .

Martin Luther King Jr.

J. K. Rowling

Amelia Earhart

Lin-Manuel Miranda